Prayer Book Studies Volume Nine

Expansive Language Liturgy, Issue 30

Edited by
Derek A. Olsen

Copyright © 2026 The Domestic and Foreign Missionary Society of the Protestant Episcopal Church in the United States of America

The English text of the liturgies presented in this book is in the public domain and is freely available for quotation without restriction.

Unless otherwise noted, Scripture quotations are from The New Revised Standard Version Bible, copyright © 1989 National Council of the Churches of Christ in the United States of America. Used by permission. All rights reserved worldwide.

Seabury Books
19 East 34th Street
New York, NY 10016
www.churchpublishing.org

Seabury Books is an imprint of Church Publishing Incorporated.

Cover design by Newgen
Typeset by Integra Software Services Pvt. Ltd.

ISBN 978-1-64065-945-2 (paperback)
ISBN 978-1-64065-946-9 (hardback)
ISBN 978-1-64065-947-6 (eBook)

Library of Congress Control Number: 2025945269

CONTENTS

Introduction v

Prayer Book Studies 30: Supplemental Liturgical Texts

Preface 3

The Daily Office 5
Concerning these Services 5
Daily Morning Prayer: Rite Two Adapted 5
An Order of Worship for the Evening *Adapted* 26
Daily Evening Prayer: Rite Two *Adapted* 30

The Holy Eucharist 41
The Word of God 41
The Holy Communion 46
The Prayers of the People 54

Musical Supplement 58
Daily Morning Prayer: Rite Two Adapted 58
Morning Prayer Canticles 60
An Order of Worship for the Evening *Adapted* 74
Daily Evening Prayer: Rite Two Adapted 78
The Holy Eucharist 79

Commentary on Prayer Book Studies 30

1. Background 103

2. Introduction 109
The ELLC Texts 111
The Daily Office 111
Morning Prayer 112
An Order of Worship for the Evening 115
Evening Prayer 116
The Holy Eucharist 116

3. Guidelines for Parish Use 126
Purpose of the Rites 126
The Importance of Education 126
Principles for Use 127
Evaluation 127
Planning and Preparation 127

4. Study Guide 128
Session One 130
Session Two 137
Session Three 143
Preparing Children for Praying with the Supplemental
    Liturgical Texts 146
Selected Portions Six Eucharistic Prayers Book of
    Common Prayer 153
Selected Portions Eucharistic Prayers Supplemental
    Liturgical Texts 155
Bibliography 156

INTRODUCTION

The Series as a Whole

The *Prayer Book Studies* (PBS) series documents the 26-year process of study and conversation that led to the adoption of the American 1979 Book of Common Prayer. It falls broadly into two parts, distinguished by the use of Roman numerals and Arabic numerals. PBS I-XVII were published by the members of the Standing Liturgical Commission between 1950 and 1966 to communicate research and draft liturgies leading toward a revision process; PBS 18-29 were published by the various drafting committees between 1970 and 1976 once the revision process was formally begun and the earlier drafts were being transformed into new usable liturgies leading up to the adoption of the new prayer book in 1979. Finally, PBS 30 and its commentary were added in 1989 to discuss inclusive and expansive language for God for further liturgical efforts.

Context of these Studies

This study and its commentary represent a new direction for the Prayer Book Studies series that has not been continued in this series since these efforts.

This material is related to and builds on 1987's *Liturgical Texts for Evaluation*, which was prepared by the Standing Liturgical Commission to begin a formal experiment with non-sexist and non-gender-specific language for God and humanity. The two studies presented here, published simultaneously in 1989, are intended to function together: PBS 30 is a booklet suitable for use in worship containing new rites that introduce inclusive and expansive language liturgies. The commentary contains the rationale, explanation, and tools for introducing these new rites to both adults and children.

While there were no further entries in the Prayer Book Studies series, the *Supplemental Liturgical Materials*—first published in 1991—continued this liturgical experimentation. The fourth edition of *Supplemental Liturgical Materials* was authorized by the 1997 General Convention as *Enriching Our Worship 1*, and subsequent releases have carried on the work begun here.

These Studies

PBS 30

This study contains no actual "study" materials at all, but the Supplemental Liturgical Texts themselves. This includes alternative Daily Office texts and canticles in direct address ("you") rather than third-person gendered pronouns ("he"). The Eucharistic material also contains alternatives to the prayer book texts and also presents two new Eucharistic prayers.

Commentary on PBS 30

The commentary contains all of the liturgical material from PBS 30 at the end of the book, but precedes it with background and introductory material, guidelines for parish use, and study guides intended to introduce both adults and children to the language and intention of the new liturgies. To avoid unnecessary reduplication, the liturgies will not be reproduced in this edition as PBS 30 may be easily consulted in the first part of the volume.

PRAYER BOOK STUDIES 30: SUPPLEMENTAL LITURGICAL TEXTS

the Standing Liturgical Commission
of the Episcopal Church

1989

Acknowledgments
The translations of the *Gloria Patri*, *Benedictus Dominus Deus*, *Magnificat*, *Te Deum laudamus*, *Gloria in excelsis*, Apostles' Creed, Lord's Prayer, Suffrages C at Morning Prayer, Nicene Creed, and *Sursum corda* used in this book are those proposed to the churches by the ecumenical English Language Liturgical Commission (ELLC). Copyright © 1987, ELLC. All rights reserved.

Grateful acknowledgment is made of the contribution of those who wrote and edited this Commentary: the Rev. Leonel L. Mitchell; the Rev. Joseph P. Russell; Sr. Jean Campbell, OSH; Mr. Howard E. Galley; the Rev. Sarah H. Motley; and the Rev. Linda S. Strohmier. The Rt. Rev. Vincent King Pettit, chair, the Standing Liturgical Commission; The Rev. Canon Lloyd S. Casson, chair, the Committee on Supplemental Liturgical Texts

PREFACE

The language of Christian liturgical prayer springs from the deep wells of Scripture, tradition, and human experience—constantly changing and complex. The liturgies of the Church have always drawn from many sources to communicate and celebrate the truth of our lives in Jesus Christ in the clearest, most compelling way possible. The effectiveness and endurability of prayer is contingent upon how well its images, words, and metaphors convey both the depth and mystery of the Gospel, and the voice and heart of the worshiping community. The common prayer of the Church emerges from the faith community and in turn, the community is formed and shaped by that prayer.

The services in Prayer Book Studies 30—Supplemental Liturgical Texts also have as their source these distinct but entirely linked currents of prayer. While the Offices and Holy Eucharist will be readily recognized as familiar forms of Anglican prayer, structured in familiar sequence, they also reflect the increasing sensitivity of the English language itself that certain words, images, and phrases are changing in meaning, particularly those which contain reference to gender. And, importantly, they also reflect substantive biblical study that has begun to awaken the Church to a wealth of images and metaphors for God which have not previously been articulated in the liturgy.

These texts, then, contain much that is familiar; some revisions which render biblical passages closer to the wording of the original language; and additional biblical images and passages which provide An expanded sense of the person of God and the worshiping community. In so doing, they engage the Church in the privilege and responsibility which every generation has to search for and speak of the evolving human experience in its relationship to the permanent truths of God. Such searching, which is the heart of the spiritual life, cannot help but be reflected in the language with which the prayer is offered.

Nowhere is the sensitivity to the basic truth that every human being is created in the image of God as important as in the liturgy of the Church. The Gospel's call—and the Church's commitment—is to speak the word of grace and, in turn, to give voice to those who receive it. These services are part of the Church's age-old effort to raise up ever-new forms of prayer and praise from every corner of life. They seek to offer new ways of speaking the old truths: an invitation to venture into the deepening prayer life of the Church and into the renewing streams of salvation.

NOTE

All worshipers, and especially every liturgical leader, are invited and urged to participate in the continuing refinement of these services. They are provided as part of an on-going dialogue in the Church, under the direction of the Standing Liturgical Commission, about language and liturgy. In their present form, they are to be used under the authority of the diocesan bishop, whose office has further information regarding the evaluation process.

A full commentary on the texts has been published separately, with chapters containing material on the liturgical and theological background for the texts, rationales and biblical references, suggested guidelines, and a brief educational program. Use of this Commentary is strongly urged for greater understanding of these services. It may be purchased by contacting the Church Hymnal Corporation (800 Second Avenue, New York, New York 10017, 1-800-223-6602) or through Church bookstores.

The Daily Office

Concerning these Services

The forms of Daily Morning and Evening Prayer and Order of Worship for the Evening which follow are intended to manifest the emerging consensus that liturgical language should be as widely inclusive and representative of the variety of the human community as possible. They are not newly composed but are adaptations of the forms in the Book of Common Prayer. In many cases both the familiar Prayer Book forms and suggested alternatives are printed in the text, so that either may be used.

The majority of texts traditionally associated with Morning and Evening Prayer find their source in the Bible. The Psalms and most of the Canticles originate there; the appointed readings are also drawn from Scripture. Even the prayers of the Offices echo biblical texts. Often the language of the biblical translations used in the liturgy is not accurately translated, and therefore less inclusive than the wording of the original text. The work of adaptation has involved finding better translations of existing texts, and including new biblical texts.

For this adaptation it was determined that language referring to the human community should express inclusivity in all instances. For example, masculine pronouns are no longer used in phrases of general human reference.

Regarding language used in reference to God, the primary concern has been that of fidelity to biblical language. The biblical metaphors of *Father* and *Lord* have a fundamental place in Christian prayer and theology and have been retained, although their use is less frequent than in existing Prayer Book services. Other Scriptural images of God, including feminine images from the Wisdom literature, have been introduced.

"Honor and glory" is an alternative doxology expressing the praise of the Triune God which may be used in place of the Gloria Patri.

Canticle numbers ending with *A* identify adaptations of the Canticles with the corresponding number in the Book of Common Prayer. Canticles 21 and 22 are additions taken from the Wisdom literature.

Additional directions are on page 40.

Please see also Commentary on Prayer Book Studies 30, a companion volume, for background and reference material about these services.

Daily Morning Prayer: Rite Two Adapted

The Officiant begins the service with one or more of these sentences of Scripture, or with one of the versicles on pages 9-10.

(The sentences and invitatory antiphons marked with an asterisk [*] are especially recommended for use with these services.)

Advent

Watch, for you do not know when the master of the house will come, in the evening, or at midnight, or at cockcrow, or in the morning, lest he come suddenly and find you asleep. *Mark 13:35, 36*

In the wilderness prepare the way of the LORD, make straight in the desert a highway for our God. *Isaiah 40:3*

The glory of the LORD shall be revealed, and all flesh shall see it together. *Isaiah 40:5*

* Arise, O Jerusalem, stand upon the height and look toward the east, and see your children gathered from west and east at the word of the Holy One. *Baruch 5:5*

Christmas

Behold, I bring you good news of a great joy which will come to all the people; for to you is born this day in the city of David, a Savior, who is Christ the Lord. *Luke 2:10,11*

Behold, the dwelling of God is with humankind. He will dwell with them, and they shall be his people, and God himself will be with them, and be their God. *Revelation 21:3*

* The Word became flesh and dwelt among us, full of grace and truth. *John 1:14*

Epiphany

Nations shall come to your light, and kings to the brightness of your rising. *Isaiah 60:3*

* I will give you as a light to the nations, that my salvation may reach to the end of the earth. *Isaiah 49:6b*

From the rising of the sun to its setting my Name shall be great among the nations, and in every place incense shall be offered to my Name, and a pure offering; for my Name shall be great among the nations, says the LORD of hosts. *Malachi 1:11*

Lent

* If we say we have no sin, we deceive ourselves, and the truth is not in us, but if we confess our sins, God, who is faithful and just, will forgive our sins and cleanse us from all unrighteousness. *1 John 1:8, 9*

Rend your hearts and not your garments. Return to the Lord your God, for he is gracious and merciful, slow to anger and abounding in steadfast love, and repents of evil. *Joel 2:13*

I will arise and go to my father, and I will say to him, "Father, I have sinned against heaven and before you; I am no longer worthy to be called your son." *Luke 15:18, 19*

To the Lord our God belong mercy and forgiveness, because we have rebelled against him and have not obeyed the voice of the Lord our God by following his laws which he set before us. *Daniel 9:9, 10*

Jesus said: "If any of you would come after me, deny yourself and take up your cross and follow me." *Mark 8:34*

Holy Week

All we like sheep have gone astray; we have turned every one to his own way; and the Lord has laid on him the iniquity of us all. *Isaiah 53:6*

Is it nothing to you, all you who pass by? Look and see if there is any sorrow like my sorrow which was brought upon me, whom the Lord has afflicted. *Lamentations 1:12*

* Christ Jesus, being found in human form, humbled himself and became obedient unto death, even death on a cross. *Philippians 2:8*

Easter Season, including Ascension Day and the Day of Pentecost

Alleluia! Christ is risen.
The Lord is risen indeed. Alleluia!

On this day the Lord has acted; we will rejoice and be glad in it. *Psalm 118:24*

Thanks be to God, who gives us the victory through our Lord Jesus Christ. *1 Corinthians 15:57*

* If then you have been raised with Christ, seek the things that are above, where Christ is, seated at the right hand of God. *Colossians 3:1*

* Christ has entered, not into a sanctuary made with hands, a copy of the true one, but into heaven itself, now to appear in the presence of God on our behalf. *Hebrews 9:24*

* You shall receive power when the Holy Spirit has come upon you; and you shall be my witnesses in Jerusalem, and in all Judea, and Samaria, and to the ends of the earth. *Acts 1:8*

Trinity Sunday

* Holy, holy, holy is the Lord God Almighty, who was, and is, and is to come! *Revelation 4:8*

All Saints and other Major Saints' Days

We give thanks to the Father, who has made us worthy to share in the inheritance of the saints in light. Colossians 1:12

* You are no longer strangers and sojourners, but citizens together with the saints and members of the household of God. *Ephesians 2:19*

* Their sound has gone out into all lands, and their message to the ends of the world. *Psalm 19:4*

Occasions of Thanksgiving

Give thanks to the LORD, and call upon his Name; make known his deeds among the peoples. *Psalm 105:1*

* We give you thanks, O God, we give you thanks, calling upon your Name and declaring all your wonderful deeds. *Psalm 75:1*

At any Time

Grace to you and peace from God our Father and the Lord Jesus Christ. *Philippians 1:2*

I was glad when they said to me, "Let us go to the house of the LORD." *Psalm 122:1*

Let the words of my mouth and the meditation of my heart be acceptable in your sight, O LORD, my strength and my redeemer. *Psalm 19:14*

"Send out your light and your truth, that they may lead me, and bring me to your holy hill and to your dwelling. *Psalm 43:3*

The LORD is in his holy temple; let all the earth keep silence before him. *Habakkuk 2:20*

The hour is coming, and now is, when the true worshipers will worship the Father in spirit and truth, for such the Father seeks to worship him. *John 4:23*

* Thus says the high and lofty One who inhabits eternity, whose name is Holy, "I dwell in the high and holy place and also with the one who has a contrite and humble spirit, to revive the spirit of the humble and to revive the heart of the contrite." *Isaiah 57:15*

* God is Spirit, and those who worship must worship in spirit and in truth. *John 4:24*

The following Confession of Sin may then be said; or the Office may continue at once with one of the versicles on pages 9-10.

Beloved in Christ, we have come together to proclaim God's praise, to hear God's holy Word, and to ask, for ourselves and on behalf of others, those things that are necessary for our life and our salvation. And so that we may prepare ourselves in heart and mind to worship God, let us kneel in silence, and with penitent and obedient hearts confess our sins, that by divine goodness and mercy we may obtain forgiveness.

or the following

Let us confess our sins against God and our neighbor.

Silence may be kept.

Officiant and People together, all kneeling

Most merciful God,
we confess that we have sinned against you
in thought, word, and deed,
by what we have done,
and by what we have left undone.
We have not loved you with our whole heart;
we have not loved our neighbors as ourselves.
We are truly sorry and we humbly repent.
For the sake of our Savior Jesus Christ,
have mercy on us and forgive us;
that we may delight in your will,
and walk in your ways,
to the glory of your Name. Amen.

The Priest alone stands and says

Almighty God have mercy on you, forgive you all your sins through the grace of Jesus Christ, strengthen you in all goodness, and by the power of the Holy Spirit keep you in eternal life. *Amen.*

A deacon or lay person using the preceding form remains kneeling, and substitutes "us" for "you" and "our" for "your."

The Invitatory and Psalter

All stand

Officiant	O God, let our mouth proclaim your praise.
People	And your glory all the day long.

or the following

Officiant	Lord, open our lips.
People	And our mouth shall proclaim your praise.

Officiant and People

Glory to the Father, and to the Son, and to the Holy Spirit; as it was in the beginning, is now, and will be for ever. Amen.

Except in Lent, add Alleluia.

or this

Honor and glory to the holy and undivided Trinity, God who creates, redeems, and inspires: One in Three and Three in One, for ever and ever. Amen.

Except in Lent, add Alleluia.

Then follows one of the Invitatory Psalms, Venite or Jubilate.

One of the following Antiphons may be sung or said with the Venite or Jubilate.

In Advent

* Our God and Savior now draws near: O come let us worship.

On the twelve days of Christmas

* Alleluia. To us a child is born: O come let us worship.

From the Epiphany through the Baptism of Christ, and on the Feasts of the Transfiguration and Holy Cross

* Christ has shown forth his glory: O come let us worship.

In Lent

Our God is full of compassion and mercy: O come let us worship.

or the following

* Today, if you would hear God's voice: harden not your hearts.

From Easter Day until the Ascension

Alleluia. The Lord is risen indeed: O come let us worship. Alleluia.

or this

* Alleluia. Christ is risen: O come let us worship. Alleluia.

From Ascension Day until the Day of Pentecost

* Alleluia. Christ the Lord has ascended into heaven: O come let us worship. Alleluia.

On the Day of Pentecost

* Alleluia. The Spirit of God renews the face of the earth: O come let us worship. Alleluia.

On Trinity Sunday

* The holy and undivided Trinity, one God: O come let us worship.

On other Sundays

* Christ has triumphed over death: 0 come let us worship.

On other Sundays and weekdays

The earth is the Lord's, for he made it: O come let us worship.

or this

Worship the Lord in the beauty of holiness: O come let us worship.

or this

The mercy of the Lord is everlasting: O come let us worship.

or the following

* God is the Rock of our salvation: O come let us worship.

or this

* The Holy One is in our midst: O come let us worship.

The alleluias in the following Antiphons are used only in Easter Season.

On Feasts of the Incarnation

* [Alleluia.] The Word was made flesh and dwelt among us: O come let us worship. [Alleluia.]

On All Saints and other Major Saints' Days

* [Alleluia.] Our God is glorious in all the saints: O come let us worship. [Alleluia.]

Venite *Psalm 95:1-7*

Come, let us sing to the Lord, *
    let us shout for joy to the Rock of our salvation.
Let us come before his presence with thanksgiving *
    and raise a loud shout to him with psalms.

For the Lord is a great God, *
    and a great King above all gods.
In his hand are the caverns of the earth, *
    and the heights of the hills are his also.
The sea is his, for he made it, *
    and his hands have molded the dry land.

Come, let us bow down, and bend the knee, *
    and kneel before the Lord our Maker.
For he is our God,
and we are the people of his pasture and the sheep of his hand. *
    Oh, that today you would hearken to God's voice!

or Psalm 95, Prayer Book, page 724

Jubilate *Psalm 100*

[Book of Common Prayer, page 82]

In place of an Invitatory Psalm, the following Morning Psalm may be sung or said.

Psalm 63 *Deus, Deus meus*

O God, you are my God; eagerly I seek you; * my soul thirsts for you, my flesh faints for you,
    as in a barren and dry land where there is no water.
Therefore I have gazed upon you in your holy place, *
    that I might behold your power and your glory.
For your loving-kindness is better than life itself; *
    my lips shall give you praise.
So will I bless you as long as I live *
    and lift up my hands in your Name.
My soul is content, as with marrow and fatness, *
    and my mouth praises you with joyful lips,
When I remember you upon my bed, *
    and meditate on you in the night watches.
For you have been my helper, *
    and under the shadow of your wings I will rejoice.

My soul clings to you; *
>   your right hand holds me fast.

>   *In Easter Week, in place of an Invitatory Psalm, or Psalm 63, the following is sung or said. It may also be used daily until the Day of Pentecost.*

Christ our Passover *Pascha nostrum*

>   1 Corinthians 5:7-8; Romans 6:9-11; 1 Corinthians 15:20-22

[Book of Common Prayer, page 83]

>   *Then follows*

The Psalm or Psalms Appointed

>   *At the end of the Psalms is sung or said*

Glory to the Father, and to the Son, and to the Holy Spirit; as it was in the beginning, is now, and will be for ever. Amen.

>   *or this*

Honor and glory to the holy and undivided Trinity, *
>   God who creates, redeems, and inspires:
One in Three and Three in One, *
>   for ever and ever. Amen.

The Lessons

>   *One or two Lessons, as appointed, are read, the Reader first saying*

A Reading (Lesson) from _____.

>   *A citation giving chapter and verse may be added.*

>   *After each Lesson the Reader may say*

	The Word of the Lord.
Answer	Thanks be to God.

>   *Or the Reader may say*   Here ends the Lesson (Reading).

>   *Silence may be kept after each Reading. One of the following Canticles or one of the Canticles found on pages 8S-96 of the Book of Common Prayer is sung*

or said after each Reading. If three Lessons are used, the Lesson from the Gospel is read after the second Canticle.

9A The First Song of Isaiah *Ecce, Deus*
Isaiah 12:2-6

Surely, it is God who saves me; *
    I will trust and will not be afraid.
For the Lord is my stronghold and my sure defense, *
    and he will be my Savior.
Therefore you shall draw water with rejoicing *
    from the springs of salvation.
And on that day you shall say, *
    Give thanks to the Lord and call upon his Name;
Make his deeds known among the peoples; *
    see that they remember that his Name is exalted.
Sing the praises of the Lord, for he has done great things, *
    and this is known in all the world.
Cry aloud, inhabitants of Zion, ring out your joy, *
    for the great one in the midst of you is the Holy One of Israel.

12A A Song of Creation *Benedicite, omnia opera Domini*
Song of the Three Young Men, 35-65

> One or more sections of this Canticle may be used. Whatever the selection, it begins with the Invocation and concludes with the Doxology.

Invocation

Glorify the Lord, all you works of the Lord, *
    sing praise and give honor for ever.
In the high vault of heaven, glorify the Lord, *
    sing praise and give honor for ever.

I The Cosmic Order

Glorify the Lord, you angels and all powers of the Lord, *
    O heavens and all waters above the heavens.
Sun and moon and stars of the sky, glorify the Lord, *
    sing praise and give honor for ever.

Glorify the Lord, every shower of rain and fall of dew, *
    all winds and fire and heat.
Winter and summer, glorify the Lord, *
    sing praise and give honor for ever.

Glorify the Lord, O chill and cold, *
    drops of dew and flakes of snow.
Frost and cold, ice and sleet, glorify the Lord, *
    sing praise and give honor for ever.

Glorify the Lord, O nights and days, *
    O shining light and enfolding dark.
Storm clouds and thunderbolts, glorify the Lord, *
    sing praise and give honor for ever.

II The Earth and its Creatures

Let the earth glorify the Lord, *
    sing praise and give honor for ever.
Glorify the Lord, O mountains and hills, and all that grows upon the earth, *
    sing praise and give honor for ever.

Glorify the Lord, O springs of water, seas, and streams, *
    O whales and all that move in the waters.
All birds of the air, glorify the Lord, *
    sing praise and give honor for ever.

Glorify the Lord, O beasts of the wild, *
    and all you flocks and herds.
O men and women everywhere, glorify the Lord, *
    sing praise and give honor for ever.

III The People of God

Let the people of God glorify the Lord, *
    sing praise and give honor for ever.
Glorify the Lord, O priests and servants of the Lord, *
    sing praise and give honor for ever.

Glorify the Lord, O spirits and souls of the righteous, *
    sing praise and give honor for ever.
You that are holy and humble of heart, glorify the Lord, *
    sing praise and give honor for ever.

Doxology

Let us glorify the Lord: Father, Son, and Holy Spirit; *
    sing praise and give honor for ever.
In the high vault of heaven, glorify the Lord, *
    sing praise and give honor for ever.

13A A Song of Praise *Benedictus es, Domine*
Song of the Three Young Men, 29-34

Glory to you, Lord God of our forebears; *
    you are worthy of praise; glory to you.
Glory to you for the radiance of your holy Name; *
    we will praise you and highly exalt you for ever.

Glory to you in the splendor of your temple; *
    on the throne of your majesty, glory to you.
Glory to you, seated between the Cherubim; *
    we will praise you and highly exalt you for ever.

Glory to you, beholding the depths; *
    in the high vault of heaven, glory to you.
Glory to you, Father, Son, and Holy Spirit; *
    we will praise you and highly exalt you for ever.

14A A Song of Penitence *Kyrie Pantokrator*
Prayer of Manasseh, 1-2, 4, 6-7, 11-15

Especially suitable in Lent, and on other penitential occasions

O Lord and Ruler of the hosts of heaven, *
    God of Abraham, Isaac, and Jacob,
    and of all their righteous offspring:
You made the heavens and the earth, *
    with all their vast array.
All things quake with fear at your presence; *
    they tremble because of your power.
But your merciful promise is beyond all measure; *
    it surpasses all that our minds can fathom.
O Most High, you are full of compassion, *
    long-suffering and abounding in mercy.
You hold back your hand; *
    you do not punish as we deserve.
In your great goodness, Lord,
you have promised forgiveness to sinners, *
    that they may repent of their sin and be saved.
And now, I bend the knee of my heart, *
    and make my appeal, sure of your gracious goodness.
I have sinned, O Lord, I have sinned, *
    and I know my wickedness only too well.
Therefore I make this prayer to you: *

Forgive me, Lord, forgive me.
Do not let me perish in my sin, *
    nor condemn me to the depths of the earth.
For you, O Lord, are the God of those who repent, *
    and in me you will show forth your goodness.
Unworthy as I am, you will save me,
in accordance with your great mercy, *
    and I will praise you without ceasing all the days of my life.
For all the powers of heaven sing your praises, *
    and yours is the glory to ages of ages. Amen.

15A The Song of Mary *Magnificat*
Luke 1:46-55

My soul proclaims the greatness of the Lord,
my spirit rejoices in God my Savior, *
    for you, Lord, have looked with favor on your lowly servant.
From this day all generations will call me blessed: *
    you, the Almighty, have done great things for me,
    and holy is your name.
You have mercy on those who fear you *
    from generation to generation.
You have shown strength with your arm *
    and scattered the proud in their conceit,
Casting down the mighty from their thrones *
    and lifting up the lowly.
You have filled the hungry with good things *
    and sent the rich away empty.
You have come to the aid of your servant Israel, *
    to remember the promise of mercy,
The promise made to our forebears, *
    to Abraham and his children for ever.

16A The Song of Zechariah *Benedictus Dominus Deus*
Luke 1:68-79

Blessed are you, Lord, the God of Israel, *
    you have come to your people and set them free.
You have raised up for us a mighty Savior, *
    born of the house of your servant David.
Through your holy prophets you promised of old
to save us from our enemies, *
    from the hands of all who hate us.

To show mercy to our forebears, *
    and to remember your holy covenant.
This was the oath you swore to our father Abraham: *
    to set us free from the hands of our enemies,
Free to worship you without fear, *
    holy and righteous before you,
    all the days of our life.
And you, child, shall be called the prophet of the Most High, *
    for you will go before the Lord to prepare the way,
To give God's people knowledge of salvation *
    by the forgiveness of their sins.
In the tender compassion of our God *
    the dawn from on high shall break upon us,
To shine on those who dwell in darkness and the shadow of death, *
    and to guide our feet into the way of peace.

18A A Song to the Lamb *Dignus es*
Revelation 4:11; 5:9-10, 13

Splendor and honor and royal power *
    are yours by right, O God Most High,
For you created everything that is, *
    and by your will they were created and have their being;

And yours by right, O Lamb that was slain, *
    for with your blood you have redeemed for God,
From every family, language, people, and nation, *
    a royal priesthood to serve our God.

And so, to the One who sits upon the throne, *
    and to Christ the Lamb,
Be worship and praise, dominion and splendor, *
    for ever and for evermore.

20A Glory to God *Gloria in excelsis*

Glory to God in the highest,
    and peace to God's people on earth.
Lord God, heavenly King,
almighty God and Father,
    we worship you, we give you thanks,
    we praise you for your glory.

Lord Jesus Christ, only Son of the Father,
Lord God, Lamb of God,
you take away the sin of the world:
> have mercy on us;
you are seated at the right hand of the Father:
> receive our prayer.
For you alone are the Holy One,
you alone are the Lord,
you alone are the Most High,
> Jesus Christ,
> with the Holy Spirit,
> in the glory of God the Father. Amen.

21A You are God *Te Deum laudamus*

We praise you, O God,
we acclaim you as Lord;
all creation worships you,
the Father everlasting.
To you all angels, all the powers of heaven,
the cherubim and seraphim, sing in endless praise:
> Holy, holy, holy Lord, God of power and might,
> heaven and earth are full of your glory.
The glorious company of apostles praise you.
The noble fellowship of prophets praise you.
The white-robed army of martyrs praise you.
Throughout the world the holy Church acclaims you:
> Father, of majesty unbounded,
> > your true and only Son, worthy of all praise,
> > the Holy Spirit, advocate and guide.
You, Christ, are the king of glory,
the eternal Son of the Father.
When you took our flesh to set us free
you humbly chose the Virgin's womb.
You overcame the sting of death
and opened the kingdom of heaven to all believers.
You are seated at God's right hand in glory.
We believe that you will come to be our judge.
> Come then, Lord, and help your people,
> bought with the price of your own blood,
> and bring us with your saints
> to glory everlasting.

22 A Song of Wisdom *Sapientia liberavit*
Wisdom 10:15-19, 20b-21

Wisdom freed from a nation of oppressors *
　　a holy people and a blameless race.
She entered the soul of a servant of the Lord, *
　　withstood dread rulers with wonders and signs.
To the saints she gave the reward of their labors, *
　　and led them by a marvelous way;
She was their shelter by day *
　　and a blaze of stars by night.
She brought them across the Red Sea, *
　　she led them through mighty waters;
But their enemies she swallowed in the waves *
　　and spewed them out from the depths of the abyss.
And then, Lord, the righteous sang hymns to your Name, *
　　and praised with one voice your protecting hand;
For Wisdom opened the mouths of the mute, *
　　and gave speech to the tongues of a new-born people.

23 A Song of Pilgrimage *Priusquam errarem*
Ecclesiasticus 51:13-22

Before I ventured forth,
even while I was very young, *
　　I sought wisdom openly in my prayer.
In the forecourts of the temple I asked for her, *
　　and I will seek her to the end.
From first blossom to early fruit, *
　　she has been the delight of my heart.
My foot has kept firmly to the true path,
　　diligently from my youth have I pursued her.
I inclined my ear a little and received her; *
　　I found for myself much wisdom and became adept in her.
To the one who gives me wisdom will I give glory, *
　　for I have resolved to live according to her way.
I have been zealous for the good, *
　　in order that I might not be put to shame.
My soul has been subdued by her, *
　　and I have been careful in my conduct.
I spread out my hands to the heavens, *
　　and lamented my ignorance of her.
I directed my soul to her, *
　　and through purification have I found her.

From the beginning I gained courage from her, *
    therefore I will not be forsaken.
In my inmost being have I been stirred to seek her, *
    therefore have I gained a good possession.
As my reward the Almighty has given me the gift of language, *
    and with it will I offer praise to God.

The Apostles' Creed

Officiant and People together, all standing

I believe in God, the Father almighty,
    creator of heaven and earth.
I believe in Jesus Christ, God's only Son, our Lord,
    who was conceived by the Holy Spirit,
    born of the Virgin Mary,
    suffered under Pontius Pilate,
    was crucified, died, and was buried;
    he descended to the dead.
    On the third day he rose again;
    he ascended into heaven,
    he is seated at the right hand of the Father,
    and he will come again to judge the living and the dead.
I believe in the Holy Spirit,
    the holy catholic Church,
    the communion of saints,
    the forgiveness of sins,
    the resurrection of the body,
    and the life everlasting. Amen.

The Prayers

The people stand or kneel

Officiant	Hear our cry, O God.
Answer	And listen to our prayer.
Officiant	Let us pray.

or this

Officiant	The Lord be with you.
Answer	And also with you.
Priest	Let us pray.

Officiant and People

Our Father in heaven,
    hallowed be your Name,
    your kingdom come,
    your will be done,
    on earth as in heaven.
Give us today our daily bread.
Forgive us our sins
    as we forgive those who sin against us.
Save us from the time of trial, and deliver us from evil.
For the kingdom, the power, and the glory are yours,
    now and for ever. Amen.

Then follows one of these sets of Suffrages

A

V. Show us your mercy, O Lord;
R. And grant us your salvation.
V. Clothe your ministers with righteousness;
R. Let your people sing with joy.
V. Give peace, O Lord, in all the world;
R. For only in you can we live in safety.
V. Lord, keep this nation under your care;
R. And guide us in the way of justice and truth.
V. Let your way be known upon earth;
R. Your saving health among all nations.
V. Let not the needy, O Lord, be forgotten;
R. Nor the hope of the poor be taken away.
V. Create in us clean hearts, O God;
R. And sustain us with your Holy Spirit.

B

V. Help us, O God our Savior;
R. Deliver us and forgive us our sins.
V. Look upon your congregation;
R. Give to your people the blessing of peace.
V. Declare your glory among the nations;
R. And your wonders among all peoples.
V. Let not the oppressed be shamed and turned away;
R. Never forget the lives of your poor.
V. Continue your loving-kindness to those who know you;

R. And your favor to those who are true of heart.
V. Satisfy us by your loving-kindness in the morning;
R. So shall we rejoice and be glad all the days of our life.

C

V. Save your people, Lord, and bless your inheritance;
R. Govern and uphold them now and always.
V. Day by day we bless you;
R. We praise your Name for ever.
V. Keep us today, Lord, from all sin.
R. Have mercy on us, Lord, have mercy.
V. Lord, show us your love and mercy;
R. For we have put our trust in you,
V. In you, Lord, is our hope;
R. Let us never be put to shame.

The Officiant then says one or more of the following Collects

The Collect of the Day

A Collect for Sundays

O God, you make us glad with the weekly remembrance of the glorious resurrection of your Son: Give us this day such blessing through our worship of you, that the week to come may be spent in your favor; through Jesus Christ our Lord. *Amen.*

A Collect for Fridays

Almighty God, whose most dear Son went not up to joy but first he suffered pain, and entered not into glory before he was crucified: Mercifully grant that we, walking in the way of the cross, may find it none other than the way of life and peace; through Jesus Christ our Savior. *Amen.*

A Collect for Saturdays

Almighty God, who after the creation of the world rested from all your works and sanctified a day of rest for all your creatures: Grant that we, putting away all earthly anxieties, may be duly prepared for the service of your sanctuary, and that our rest here upon earth may be a preparation for the eternal rest promised to your people in heaven; through Jesus Christ our Savior. *Amen.*

A Collect for the Renewal of Life

Eternal God, whose light divides the day from the night and turns the shadow of death into the morning: Drive far from us all wrong desires, incline our hearts to keep your law, and guide our feet into the way of peace; that, having done your will with cheerfulness during the day, we may, when night comes, rejoice to give you thanks; through Jesus Christ our Savior. *Amen.*

A Collect for Peace

O God, the author of peace and lover of concord, to know you is eternal life and to serve you is perfect freedom: Defend us, your humble servants, in all assaults of our enemies; that we, surely trusting in your defense, may not fear the power of any adversaries; through the might of Jesus Christ our Lord. *Amen.*

A Collect for Grace

Almighty and everlasting God, you have brought us in safety to this new day: preserve us with your mighty power, that we may not fall into sin, nor be overcome by adversity; and in all we do, direct us to the fulfilling of your purpose; through Jesus Christ our Savior. *Amen.*

A Collect for Guidance

O God, our Creator and Sustainer, in you we live and move and have our being: We humbly pray you so to guide and govern us by your Holy Spirit, that in all the cares and occupations of our life we may not forget you, but may remember that we are ever walking in your sight; through Jesus Christ our Lord. *Amen.*

Then, unless the Eucharist or a form of general intercession is to follow, one of the following prayers for mission is added

Almighty and everlasting God, by whose Spirit the whole body of your faithful people is governed and sanctified: Receive our supplications and prayers which we offer before you for all members of your holy Church, that in their vocation and ministry they may truly and devoutly serve you; through our Lord and Savior Jesus Christ. *Amen.*

or the following

O God, you have made of one blood all the peoples of the earth, and sent your blessed Son to preach peace to those who are far off and to those who are near: Grant that people everywhere may seek after you and find you; bring the nations into your fold; pour out your Spirit upon all flesh; and hasten the coming of your kingdom; through Jesus Christ our Lord. *Amen.*

or this

Lord Jesus Christ, you stretched out your arms of love on the hard wood of the cross that everyone might come within the reach of your saving embrace: So clothe us in your Spirit that we, reaching forth our hands in love, may bring those who do not know you to the knowledge and love of you; for the honor of your Name. *Amen.*

Here may be sung a hymn or anthem.

Authorized intercessions and thanksgivings may follow.

Before the close of the Office one or both of the following may be used

The General Thanksgiving

Officiant and People

Almighty God, Father of all mercies,
we your unworthy servants give you humble thanks
for all your goodness and loving-kindness
to us and to all whom you have made.
We bless you for our creation, preservation,
and all the blessings of this life;
but above all for your immeasurable love
in the redemption of the world by our Lord Jesus Christ;
for the means of grace, and for the hope of glory.
And, we pray, give us such an awareness of your mercies,
that with truly thankful hearts we may show forth your praise,
not only with our lips, but in our lives,
by giving up our selves to your service,
and by walking before you
in holiness and righteousness all our days;
through Jesus Christ our Lord,
to whom, with you and the Holy Spirit,
be honor and glory throughout all ages. Amen.

A Prayer of St. Chrysostom

Jesus our Savior, you have given us grace at this time with one accord to make our common supplication to you; and you have promised that when two or three are agreed in your Name you will grant their requests: Fulfill now, 0 Lord, our desires and petitions as may be best for us; granting us in this world knowledge of your truth, and in the age to come life everlasting. *Amen.*

Then may be said

Let us bless the Lord.
Thanks be to God.

From Easter Day through the Day of Pentecost "Alleluia, alleluia" may be added to the preceding versicle and response.

The Officiant may then conclude with one of the following

The grace of our Lord Jesus Christ, and the love of God, and the fellowship of the Holy Spirit, be with us all evermore. *Amen. 2 Corinthians 13:14*

May the God of hope fill us with all joy and peace in believing through the power of the Holy Spirit. *Amen. Romans 15:13*

Glory to God whose power, working in us, can do infinitely more than we can ask or imagine: Glory to God from generation to generation in the Church, and in Christ Jesus for ever and ever. *Amen. Ephesians 3:20, 21*

An Order of Worship for the Evening Adapted

The church is dark, or partially so, when the service is to begin.

All stand, and the Officiant greets the people with these words

	Light and peace, in Jesus Christ our Lord.
People	Thanks be to God.

In place of the above, from Easter Day through the Day of Pentecost

Officant	Christ has risen as he promised. Alleluia!
People	And has appeared to the disciples. Alleluia!

or this

Officant	Stay with us, Christ, for it is evening. Alleluia!
People	Illumine your Church with your radiance. Alleluia!

In Lent and on other penitential occasions

Officant	Blessed be the God of our salvation.
People	Who bears our burdens and forgives our sins.

One of the following, or some other Short Lesson of Scripture appropriate to the occasion or to the season, may then be read

Jesus said, "You are the light of the world. A city built on a hill cannot be hid. No one lights a lamp to put it under a bucket, but on a lamp-stand where it gives light for everyone in the house. And you, like the lamp, must shed light among other people, so that they may see the good you do, and give glory to your Father in heaven." *Matthew 5:14-16*

What we preach is not ourselves, but Jesus Christ as Lord, with ourselves as your servants for Jesus' sake. For it is the God who said, "Let light shine out of darkness;' who has shone in our hearts to give the light of knowledge of the glory of God in the face of Christ. *2 Corinthians 4:5-6*

If I say, "Surely the darkness will cover me, sand the light around me turn to night," darkness is not dark to you, O God; the night is as bright as the day; darkness and light to you are both alike. *Psalm 1-39:10-11*

The Officiant then says the Prayer for Light, using any one of the following or some other suitable prayer, first saying

Let us pray.

Almighty God, we give you thanks for surrounding us, as daylight fades, with the brightness of the vesper light; and we implore you of your great mercy that, as you enfold us with the radiance of this light, so you would shine into our hearts the brightness of your Holy Spirit; through Jesus Christ our Lord. *Amen.*

Grant us, Lord, the lamp of charity which never fails, that it may burn in us and shed its light on those around us, and that by its brightness we may have a vision of that holy City, where dwells the true and never-failing Light, Jesus the Christ. *Amen.*

O Lord God Almighty, as you have taught us to call the evening, the morning, and the noonday one day; and have made the sun to know its going down: Dispel the darkness of our hearts, that by your brightness we may know you to be the true God and eternal light, living and reigning for ever and ever. *Amen.*

Be our light in the darkness, O God, and in your great mercy defend us from all perils and dangers of this night; for the love of your only Son, our Savior Jesus Christ. *Amen.*

Advent

Collect for the First Sunday of Advent

Christmas, Epiphany, and other Feasts of the Incarnation

Collect for the First Sunday after Christmas

Lent and other times of penitence

Most merciful God, kindle within us the fire of love, that by its cleansing flame we may be purged of all our sins and made worthy to worship you in spirit and in truth; through Jesus Christ our Light. *Amen.*

Easter Season

Eternal God, who led your ancient people into freedom by a pillar of cloud by day and a pillar of fire by night: Grant that we who walk in the light of your presence may rejoice in the liberty of the children of God; through Jesus Christ our Savior. Amen.

Festivals of Saints

Lord Christ, your saints have been the lights of the world in every generation: Grant that we who follow in their footsteps may be made worthy to enter with them into that heavenly country where you live and reign for ever and ever. Amen.

The candles at the Altar are now lighted, as are other candles and lamps as may be convenient.

During the candle-lighting, an appropriate anthem or psalm may be sung, or silence kept.

The following hymn, or a metrical version of it, or Psalm 134, or Psalm 141, or some other hymn, is then sung

O Gracious Light *Phos hilaron*

O gracious Light,
pure brightness of the everliving Father in heaven,
O Jesus Christ, holy and blessed!

Now as we come to the setting of the sun,
and our eyes behold the vesper light,
we sing your praises, O God: Father, Son, and Holy Spirit.

You are worthy at all times to be praised by happy voices,
O Son of God, O Giver of life, and to be glorified through all the worlds.

or this

Psalm 134 *Ecce nunc*

Behold now, bless the Lord, all you servants of the Lord, *
    you that stand by night in the house of the Lord.
Lift up your hands in the holy place and bless the Lord; *
    the Lord who made heaven and earth bless you out of Zion.

or this

Psalm 141:1-3, 8ab *Domine, clamavi*

O LORD, I call to you; come to me quickly; *
 hear my voice when I cry to you.
Let my prayer be set forth in your sight as incense, *
 the lifting up of my hands as the evening sacrifice.
Set a watch before my mouth, O LORD,
 and guard the door of my lips; *
 let not my heart incline to any evil thing.
My eyes are turned to you, Lord GOD; *
 in you I take refuge.

> *The service may then continue in any of the following ways:*
>
> *With Evening Prayer, beginning with the Psalms; or with some other Office or Devotion;*
>
> *With the celebration of the Holy Eucharist, beginning with the Salutation and Collect of the Day;*
>
> *Or, it may be followed by a meal or other activity, in which case Phos hilaron, or its alternative, may be followed by the Lord's Prayer and a grace or blessing;*
>
> *Or, it may continue as a complete evening Office with the following elements:*

Selection from the Psalter. Silence, or a suitable Collect, or both, may follow the Psalmody.

Bible Reading. A sermon or homily, a passage from Christian literature, or a brief silence, may follow the Reading.

Canticle. The Magnificat or other canticle, or some other hymn of praise.

Prayers. A litany, or other suitable devotions, including the Lord's Prayer. Blessing or Dismissal, or both. The Peace may then be exchanged.

> *On feasts or other days of special significance, the Collect of the Day, or one proper to the season, may precede the Blessing or Dismissal. On other days, either of the following, or one of the Collects from Evening Prayer or from Compline, may be so used.*

Blessed are you, O Lord our God, creator of the changes of day and night, giving rest to the weary, renewing the strength of those who are spent, bestowing upon us occasions of song in the evening. As you have protected us in the day that is past, so be with us in the coming night; keep us from every sin, every evil, and every fear; for you are our light and salvation, and the strength of our life. To you, be glory for endless ages. *Amen.*

Almighty, everlasting God, let our prayer be set forth in your sight as incense, the lifting up of our hands as the evening sacrifice. Give us grace to behold you, present in your Word and Sacraments, and to recognize you in the lives of those around us. Stir up in us the flame of that love which burned in the heart of your Son as he bore his passion, and let it burn in us to eternal life and to the ages of ages. *Amen.*

A bishop or priest may use one of the following or some other blessing or grace

The Lord bless you and keep you. *Amen.*
The Lord make his face to shine upon you
    and be gracious to you. *Amen.*
The Lord lift up his countenance upon you
    and give you peace. *Amen.*

or this

May the blessing of the God of Abraham and Sarah, and of Jesus Christ born of our sister Mary, and of the Holy Spirit, who broods over the world as a mother over her children, be upon you and remain with you always. *Amen.*

A deacon or lay person using one of the preceding blessings substitutes "us" for "you."

A Dismissal may be used (adding "Alleluia, alleluia" in Easter Season)

The People respond

Thanks be to God.

In Easter Season the People respond

Thanks be to God. Alleluia, alleluia.

Daily Evening Prayer: Rite Two *Adapted*

The Officiant begins the service with one or more of the following sentences of Scripture, or of those on pages 6-8;

or with the Service of Light on pages 26-30, and continuing with the appointed Psalmody;

or with one of the versicles on page 32.

* Let my prayer be set forth in your sight as incense, the lifting up of my hands as the evening sacrifice. *Psalm 141:2*

Grace to you and peace from God our Father and from the Lord Jesus Christ. *Philippians 1:2*

Worship the Lord in the beauty of holiness; let the whole earth tremble before him. *Psalm 96:9*

Yours is the day, O God, yours also the night; you established the moon and the sun. You fixed all the boundaries of the earth; you made both summer and winter. *Psalm 74:15, 16*

I will bless the Lord who gives me counsel; my heart teaches me, night after night. I have set the Lord always before me; because God is at my right hand, I shall not fall. *Psalm 16:7, 8*

Seek the One who made the Pleiades and Orion, and turns deep darkness into the morning, and darkens the day into night; who calls for the waters of the sea and pours them out upon the surface of the earth: The Lord is God's name. *Amos 5:8*

* If I say, "Surely the darkness will cover me, and the light around me turn to night," darkness is not dark to you, O God; the night is as bright as the day; darkness and light to you are both alike. *Psalm 139:10, 11*

Jesus said, "I am the light of the world; whoever follows me will not walk in darkness, but will have the light of life." *John 8:12*

The following Confession of Sin may then be said; or the Office may continue at once with one of the versicles on page 32.

Confession of Sin

The Officiant says to the people

Dear friends in Christ, here in the presence of Almighty God, let us kneel in silence, and with penitent and obedient hearts confess our sins, so that we may obtain forgiveness by God's infinite goodness and mercy.

or this

Let us confess our sins against God and our neighbor.

Silence may be kept.

Officiant and People together, all kneeling

Most merciful God,
we confess that we have sinned against you

in thought, word, and deed,
by what we have done,
and by what we have left undone.
We have not loved you with our whole heart;
we have not loved our neighbors as ourselves.
We are truly sorry and we humbly repent.
For the sake of our Savior Jesus Christ,
have mercy on us and forgive us;
that we may delight in your will,
and walk in your ways,
to the glory of your Name. Amen.

The priest alone stands and says

Almighty God have mercy on you, forgive you all your sins through the grace of Jesus Christ, strengthen you in all goodness, and by the power of the Holy Spirit keep you in eternal life. *Amen.*

A deacon or lay person using the preceding form remains kneeling, and substitutes "us" for "you" and "our" for "your."

The Invitatory and Psalter

All stand

Officant	O God, be not far from us.
People	Come quickly to help us, O God.

or this

Officant	O God, make speed to save us.
People	Lord, make haste to help us.

Officiant and People

Glory to the Father, and to the Son, and to the Holy Spirit; as it was in the beginning, is now, and will be for ever. Amen.

Except in Lent, add Alleluia.

or this

Honor and glory to the holy and undivided Trinity, God who creates, redeems, and inspires; One in Three and Three in One for ever and ever. Amen.

Except in Lent, add Alleluia.

One of the following, or some other suitable hymn, or an Invitatory Psalm, may be sung or said

O Gracious Light *Phos hilaron*

O gracious Light,
pure brightness of the everliving Father in heaven,
O Jesus Christ, holy and blessed!

Now as we come to the setting of the sun,
and our eyes behold the vesper light,
we sing your praises, O God: Father, Son, and Holy Spirit.

You are worthy at all times to be praised by happy voices,
O Son of God, O Giver of life,
and to be glorified through all the worlds.

or this

Psalm 134 *Ecce nunc*

Behold now, bless the Lord, all you servants of the Lord, *
    you that stand by night in the house of the Lord.
Lift up your hands in the holy place and bless the Lord; *
    the Lord who made heaven and earth bless you out of Zion.

or this

Psalm 141:1-3, 8ab *Domine, clamavi*

O Lord, I call to you; come to me quickly; *
    hear my voice when I cry to you.
Let my prayer be set forth in your sight as incense, *
    the lifting up of my hands as the evening sacrifice.
Set a watch before my mouth, O Lord,
and guard the door of my lips; *
    let not my heart incline to any evil thing.
My eyes are turned to you, Lord God; *
    in you I take refuge.

Then follows

The Psalm or Psalms Appointed

At the end of the Psalms is sung or said

Glory to the Father, and to the Son, and to the Holy Spirit; as it was in the beginning, is now, and will be for ever. Amen.

or this

Honor and glory to the holy and undivided Trinity, God who creates, redeems, and inspires; One in Three and Three in One, for ever and ever. Amen

The Lessons

One or two Lessons, as appointed, are read, the Reader first saying

A Reading (Lesson) from _____.

A citation giving chapter and verse may be added.

After each Lesson the Reader may say

               The Word of the Lord.
Answer   Thanks be to God.

Or the Reader may say   Here ends the Lesson (Reading).

Silence may be kept after each Reading. One of the following Canticles, or one of those on pages 14-21, is sung or said after each Reading. If three Lessons are used, the Lesson from the Gospel is read after the second Canticle.

The Song of Mary *Magnificat*
Luke 1:46-55

My soul proclaims the greatness of the Lord,
my spirit rejoices in God my Savior, *
    for you, Lord, have looked with favor on your lowly servant.
From this day all generations will call me blessed: *
    you, the Almighty, have done great things for me,
    and holy is your name.
You have mercy on those who fear you *
    from generation to generation.
You have shown strength with your arm *
    and scattered the proud in their conceit,

Casting down the mighty from their thrones *
    and lifting up the lowly.
You have filled the hungry with good things *
    and sent the rich away empty.
You have come to the aid of your servant Israel, *
    to remember the promise of mercy,
The promise made to our forebears, *
    to Abraham and his children for ever.

The Song of Simeon *Nunc dimittis*
Luke 2:29-32

Lord, you now have set your servant free *
    to go in peace as you have promised;
For these eyes of mine have seen the Savior, *
    whom you have prepared for all the world to see:
A Light to enlighten the nations, *
    and the glory of your people Israel.

The Apostles' Creed

Officiant and People together, all standing

I believe in God, the Father almighty,
    creator of heaven and earth.
I believe in Jesus Christ, God's only Son, our Lord,
    who was conceived by the Holy Spirit,
    born of the Virgin Mary,
    suffered under Pontius Pilate,
    was crucified, died, and was buried;
    he descended to the dead.
    On the third day he rose again;
    he ascended into heaven,
    he is seated at the right hand of the Father,
    and he will come again to judge the living and the dead.
I believe in the Holy Spirit,
    the holy catholic Church,
    the communion of saints,
    the forgiveness of sins,
    the resurrection of the body,
    and the life everlasting. Amen.

The Prayers

The people stand or kneel

Officant   Hear our cry, O God.
Answer   And listen to our prayer.
Officant   Let us pray.

or this

Officant   The Lord be with you.
Answer   And also with you.
Priest   Let us pray.

Officiant and People

Our Father in heaven,
    hallowed be your Name,
    your kingdom come,
    your will be done,
    on earth as in heaven.
Give us today our daily bread.
Forgive us our sins
    as we forgive those who sin against us.
Save us from the time of trial, and deliver us from evil.
For the kingdom, the power, and the glory are yours,
    now and for ever. Amen.

Then follows one of these sets of Suffrages

A

V. Show us your mercy, O Lord;
R. And grant us your salvation.
V. Clothe your ministers with righteousness;
R. Let your people sing with joy.
V. Give peace, O Lord, in all the world;
R. For only in you can we live in safety.
V. Lord, keep this nation under your care;
R. And guide us in the way of justice and truth.
V. Let your way be known upon earth;
R. Your saving health among all nations.
V. Let not the needy, O Lord, be forgotten;

R. Nor the hope of the poor be taken away.
V. Create in us clean hearts, O God;
R. And sustain us with your Holy Spirit.

B

That this evening may be holy, good, and peaceful,
We entreat you, O God.

That your holy angels may lead us in paths of peace and goodwill,
We entreat you, O God.

That we may be pardoned and forgiven for our sins and offenses,
We entreat you, O God.

That there may be peace to your Church and to the whole world,
We entreat you, O God.

That we may depart this life in your faith and fear, and not be condemned before the great judgment seat of Christ,
We entreat you, O God.

That we may be bound together by your Holy Spirit in the communion of [_____ and] all your saints, entrusting one another and all our life to Christ,
We entreat you, O God.

The Officiant then says one or more of the following Collects

The Collect of the Day

A Collect for Sundays

O God, whose Son our Savior Jesus Christ triumphed over the powers of death and prepared for us our place in the new Jerusalem: Grant that we, who have this day given thanks for his resurrection, may praise you in that City of which he is the light, and where he lives and reigns for ever and ever. *Amen.*

A Collect for Fridays

Lord Jesus Christ, by your death you took away the sting of death: Grant to us your servants so to follow in faith where you have led the way, that we may at length fall asleep peacefully in you and wake up in your likeness; for your tender mercies' sake. *Amen.*

A Collect for Saturdays

O God, the source of eternal light: Shed forth your unending day upon us who watch for you, that our lips may praise you, our lives may bless you, and our worship on the morrow give you glory; through Jesus Christ our Savior. *Amen.*

A Collect for Peace

Most holy God, the source of all good desires, all right judgments, and all just works: Give to us, your servants, that peace which the world cannot give, so that our minds may be fixed on the doing of your will, and that we, being delivered from the fear of all enemies, may live in peace and quietness; through the mercies of Christ Jesus our Savior. *Amen.*

A Collect for Aid against Perils

Be our light in the darkness, O God, and in your great mercy defend us from all perils and dangers of this night; for the love of your only Son, our Savior Jesus Christ. *Amen.*

A Collect for Protection

O God, the life of all who live, the light of the faithful, the strength of those who labor, and the repose of the dead: We thank you for the blessings of the day that is past, and humbly ask for your protection through the coming night. Bring us in safety to the morning hours; through him who died and rose again for us, your Son our Savior Jesus Christ. *Amen.*

A Collect for the Presence of Christ

Lord Jesus, stay with us, for evening is at hand and the day is past; be our companion in the way, kindle our hearts, and awaken hope, that we may know you as you are revealed in Scripture and the breaking of bread. Grant this for the sake of your love. *Amen.*

Then, unless the Eucharist or a form of general intercession is to follow, one of these prayers for mission is added

O God and Maker of all, whom the whole heavens adore: Let the whole earth also worship you, all nations obey you, all tongues confess and bless you, and people everywhere love you and serve you in peace; through Jesus the Christ. *Amen.*

or the following

Keep watch, dear Lord, with those who work, or watch, or weep this night, and give your angels charge over those who sleep. Tend the sick, Lord Christ; give rest to the weary, bless the dying, soothe the suffering, pity the afflicted, shield the joyous; and all for your love's sake. *Amen.*

or this

O God, you manifest in your servants the signs of your presence: Send forth upon us the Spirit of love, that in companionship with one another your abounding grace may increase among us; through Jesus the Christ. *Amen.*

Here may be sung a hymn or anthem.

Authorized intercessions and thanksgivings may follow.

Before the close of the Office one or both of the following may be used.

The General Thanksgiving

Officiant and People

Almighty God, Father of all mercies,
we your unworthy servants give you humble thanks
for all your goodness and loving-kindness
to us and to all whom you have made.
We bless you for our creation, preservation,
and all the blessings of this life;
but above all for your immeasurable love
in the redemption of the world by our Lord Jesus Christ;
for the means of grace, and for the hope of glory.
And, we pray, give us such an awareness of your mercies,
that with truly thankful hearts we may show forth your praise,
not only with our lips, but in our lives,
by giving up our selves to your service,
and by walking before you
in holiness and righteousness all our days; through Jesus Christ our Lord,
to whom, with you and the Holy Spirit,
be honor and glory throughout all ages. Amen.

A Prayer of St. Chrysostom

Jesus our Savior, you have given us grace at this time with one accord to make our common supplication to you; and you have promised that when two or three are agreed in your Name you will grant their requests: Fulfill now, O Lord, our desires and petitions as may be best for us; granting us in this world knowledge of your truth, and in the age to come life everlasting. *Amen.*

Then may be said

Let us bless the Lord.
Thanks be to God.

From Easter Day through the Day of Pentecost "Alleluia, alleluia" may be added to the preceding versicle and response.

The Officiant may then conclude with one of the following

The grace of our Lord Jesus Christ, and the love of God and the fellowship of the Holy Spirit, be with us all evermore. *Amen. 2 Corinthians 13:14*

May the God of hope fill us with all joy and peace in believing through the power of the Holy Spirit. *Amen. Romans 15:13*

Glory to God whose power, working in us, can do infinitely more than we can ask or imagine: Glory to God from generation to generation in the Church, and in Christ Jesus for ever and ever. *Amen. Ephesians 3:20, 21*

Additional Directions

Morning and Evening Prayer

Any of the opening sentences of Scripture, including those listed for specific seasons or days, may be used at any time, according to the discretion of the officiant.

The proper antiphons on pages 10-11 may be used as refrains with either of the two Invitatory Psalms, the Venite or the Jubilate.

Antiphons drawn from the Psalms themselves, or from the opening sentences given in the Offices, or from other passages of Scripture may be used with the morning Psalm 63, with the evening Psalms 134 and 141, and with the other Psalms and biblical Canticles.

The Gloria Patri or the "Honor and glory" is always sung or said at the conclusion of the entire portion of the Psalter; and may be used after the Invitatory Psalm, after the morning or evening psalm, or the Canticle "Christ our Passover," after each psalm, and after each section of Psalm 119.

After Canticles 8, 9, 9A, 10, 11, 12, 12A, 15, 15A, 16, 16A, 17, 19, 22, and 23, the Gloria Patri or the following theological equivalent may be sung or said:

Honor and glory to the holy and undivided Trinity, *
    God who creates, redeems, and inspires:
One in Three and Three in One, *
    for ever and ever. Amen.

The Additional Directions continue with "The following pointing of the Gloria..." on page 141 and all that follows on pages 142 and 143 of the Book of Common Prayer.

The directions "Concerning the Service" and "Concerning the Celebration" on pages 74 and 108 of the Prayer Book apply also to these services.

Concerning this Eucharistic Rite

This eucharistic rite is newly composed following the classical pattern and the traditional content of the ancient Christian liturgical rites. It follows the familiar order of Rite Two in the Book of Common Prayer and is to be considered a supplement to it.

The intent of this rite is to enrich our liturgical prayer by making available a fuller array of images of God. As the People of God we are called to name God in our rites as we share in the worship of the whole creation offering praise to its Source.

The rite contains two newly composed eucharistic prayers (designated *First Supplemental Eucharistic Prayer* and *Second Supplemental Eucharistic Prayer*) and two new Prayers of the People (*Prayers of the People—First Supplement and Prayers of the People—Second Supplement*). The First Supplemental Eucharistic Prayer has as its theme the creation of all people in the image of God as the source of Christian inclusiveness. The Second Supplemental Eucharistic Prayer has the central metaphor of God bringing to birth and nourishing the whole creation.

Collects which echo the themes of the eucharistic prayers are included as alternatives to the Collect of the Day from the Book of Common Prayer.

The rubrics found in Concerning the Celebration on page 354 of the Book of Common Prayer are also applicable to this rite.

Additional directions are on page 57.

Please see also Commentary on Prayer Book Studies 30, a companion volume, for background and reference material for this service.

The Holy Eucharist

The Word of God

A hymn, psalm, or anthem may be sung. The people standing, the Celebrant says

	Blessed be the one, holy, and living God.
People	Glory to God for ever and ever.

In place of the above, from Easter Day through the Day of Pentecost

Celebrant	Alleluia. Blessed be our God.
People	Christ is risen. Alleluia.

In Lent and on other penitential occasions

Celebrant	Blessed be the God of our salvation:
People	Who bears our burdens and forgives our sins.

When appointed, the following hymn or some other song of praise is sung or said, all standing

Splendor and honor and royal power
    are yours by right, O God Most High,
For you created everything that is,
    and by your will they were created and have their being;

And yours by right, O Lamb that was slain,
    for with your blood you have redeemed for God,
From every family, language, people, and nation,
    a royal priesthood to serve our God.

And so, to the One who sits upon the throne,
    and to Christ the Lamb,
Be worship and praise, dominion and splendor,
    for ever and for evermore.

On other occasions the following is used

Holy God,
Holy and Mighty,
Holy Immortal One,
Have mercy upon us.

The Collect of the Day

The Celebrant says to the people

	God be with you. *or* The Lord be with you.
People	And also with you.
Celebrant	Let us pray.

The Celebrant says the Collect of the Day or one of the following Collects

Suggested for use with First Supplemental Eucharistic Prayer

O God, who wonderfully created and yet more wonderfully restored the dignity of human nature: Guide us in your grace that we may know and live the divine life of Christ, who reveals your majesty in our humanity; through your Anointed One, who lives and reigns with you and the Holy Spirit, one God, for ever and ever. *Amen.*

or this

O God, you have breathed new life into us through your Holy Spirit: Grant that we, reborn in your Name, anointed by your Spirit, and nourished in your Body, may burn with the fire of your love throughout the world; through the Risen Christ, who lives with you and the Holy Spirit, one God, for ever and ever. *Amen.*

Suggested for use with Second Supplemental Eucharistic Prayer

O God our creator, fountain of light and love and life: Be near to us and embrace us, and teach us to walk in your truth and your ways; through Jesus Christ who reigns in glory, with you and the Holy Spirit, now and for ever. *Amen.*

The Lessons

The people sit. One or two Lessons, as appointed, are read, the Reader first saying

A Reading (Lesson) from _____.

A citation giving chapter and verse may be added.

After each Reading, the Reader may say

> The Word of the Lord.
> *People* Thanks be to God.

or the Reader may say Here ends the Reading (Epistle).

Silence may follow.

A Psalm, hymn, or anthem may follow each Reading.

Then, all standing, the Deacon or a Priest reads the Gospel, first saying

> The Holy Gospel of our Savior Jesus Christ according to _____.
> *People* Glory to you, Lord Christ.

After the Gospel, the Reader says

> The Gospel of the Lord.
> *People* Praise to you, Lord Christ.

The Sermon

On Sundays and other Major Feasts there follows, all standing

The Nicene Creed

We believe in one God, the Father, the Almighty,
    maker of heaven and earth,
    of all that is, seen and unseen.

We believe in one Lord, Jesus Christ,
    the only Son of God,
    eternally begotten of the Father,
    God from God, Light from Light,
    true God from true God,
    begotten, not made,
    of one Being with the Father;
    through him all things were made.
    For us and for our salvation
        he came down from heaven,
        was incarnate of the Holy Spirit and the Virgin Mary
        and became truly human.
        For our sake he was crucified under Pontius Pilate;
        he suffered death and was buried.
        On the third day he rose again
        in accordance with the Scriptures;
        he ascended into heaven
        and is seated at the right hand of the Father.
        He will come again in glory to judge the living and the dead,
        and his kingdom will have no end.

We believe in the Holy Spirit, the Lord, the giver of life,
    who proceeds from the Father and the Son,
    who with the Father and the Son is worshiped and glorified,
    who has spoken through the prophets.
    We believe in one holy catholic and apostolic Church.
    We acknowledge one baptism for the forgiveness of sins.
    We look for the resurrection of the dead,
        and the life of the world to come. Amen.

The Prayers Of The People

Prayer is offered with intercession for

The Universal Church, its members, and its mission
The Nation and all in authority
The welfare of the world
The concerns of the local community

Those who suffer and those in any trouble
The departed (with commemoration of a saint when appropriate)

Prayer may be offered according to one of the forms on pages 54-57 of this book, or of those in the Book of Common Prayer (pages 383-393).

Confession of Sin

A Confession of Sin is said here if it has not been said earlier. On occasion, the Confession may be omitted.

The Deacon or Celebrant says

Let us confess our sins against God, our neighbor, and ourselves.

Silence may be kept.

Minister and People

God of all mercy,
we confess that we have sinned against you,
resisting your will in our lives.
We have not honored you in ourselves, in each other,
and in the world which you have made.
Reach out your saving arm
and rescue us from our sin.
Forgive, restore, and strengthen us
through our Savior Jesus Christ,
that we may abide in your love
and serve only your will
for your people and all creation. Amen.

The Bishop when present, or the Priest, stands and says

Almighty God have mercy on you, forgive you all your sins through the grace of Jesus Christ, strengthen you in all goodness, and by the power of the Holy Spirit keep you in eternal life. *Amen.*

The Peace

All stand. The Celebrant says to the people

	The peace of Christ be always with you.
People	And also with you.

Then the Ministers and People may greet one another in the name of the Risen Christ.

The Holy Communion

The Celebrant may begin the Offertory with a sentence of Scripture.

During the Offertory, a hymn, psalm, or anthem may be sung.

Representatives of the congregation bring the people's offerings of bread and wine, and money or other gifts, to the deacon or celebrant. The people stand while the offerings are presented and placed on the Altar.

The Great Thanksgiving

A Second Supplemental form will be found on page 49.

First Supplemental Eucharistic Prayer

The people remain standing. The Celebrant, whether bishop or priest, faces them and sings or says

	The Lord be with you.
People	And also with you.
Celebrant	Lift up your hearts.
People	We lift them to the Lord.
Celebrant	Let us give thanks to the Lord our God.
People	It is right to give our thanks and praise.

Then, facing the Holy Table, the Celebrant proceeds

It is good and joyful that in your presence we give you thanks, Holy God, for you have included us in creation and made us in your glorious image. You have remembered us from our beginning and fed us with your constant love; you have redeemed us in Jesus Christ and knit us into one body. Through your Spirit you replenish us, and call us to fullness of life. Therefore, joining with angels and archangels and with all the faithful in every generation, we give voice to all creation as we sing (say):

Celebrant and People

Holy, holy, holy God of power and might,
heaven and earth are full of your glory.
    Hosanna in the highest.

Blessed is the one who comes in the name of our God.
Hosanna in the highest.

Then the Celebrant continues

Most generous, self-giving God,
we celebrate your gift of creation.
We rejoice that you have formed us in your image
and called us to dwell in your infinite love.

You gave the world into our care
that we might be your faithful stewards
and reflect your bountiful grace.
Through Abraham and Sarah
you blessed us with a holy heritage.
You delivered us from slavery,
sustained us in the wilderness,
and raised up prophets
that we might realize the fullness of your promise.

But we failed to honor your image
in one another and in ourselves;
we failed to see your goodness in the world around us;
and so we violated your creation,
abused one another,
and rejected your love.
Yet you did not abandon us to sin and death,
but sent Jesus Christ to be our Savior.

United with us by incarnation
through Mary and the Holy Spirit,
and born into the human family,
he showed us the way of freedom and life.
Walking among us,
he touched us with healing and transforming power,
and showed us your glory.
Giving himself freely to death on the cross,
he triumphed over evil and became our salvation.

At the following words concerning the bread, the Celebrant is to hold it, or lay a hand upon it; and at the words concerning the cup, to hold or place a hand upon the cup and any other vessel containing wine to be consecrated.

On the night before he died for us,
our Savior Jesus Christ took bread,

and when he had given thanks to you,
he broke it, and gave it to his friends, saying:
"Take, eat:
This is my Body which is given for you.
Do this for the remembrance of me."

After supper, Jesus took the cup of wine,
and when he had given thanks,
he gave it to them, saying:
"Drink this, all of you:
This is my Blood of the new Covenant,
poured out for you and for all for the forgiveness of sins.
Whenever you drink it, do this for the remembrance of me."

In obedience to this command, O God:

Celebrant and People

We remember his death on the cross,
We proclaim the resurrection to new life,
We await the return of Christ in glory;

The Celebrant continues

And we present to you from your creation,
this bread and this wine.
By your Holy Spirit may they become for us
the bread of life and the cup of salvation,
the Body and Blood of our Savior Jesus Christ,
that we may be Christ's Body in the world.

Remember your holy people,
and, in the fullness of time,
welcome us into the everlasting heritage
of your sons and daughters,
that with [_____ and] all your saints,
past and yet to come,
we may praise your Name for ever.

Through Christ and with Christ and in Christ,
in the unity of the Holy Spirit
all honor and glory are yours, O God,
now and for ever. *AMEN.*

Continue with the Lord's Prayer on page 51.

Second Supplemental Eucharistic Prayer

The people remain standing. The Celebrant, whether bishop or priest, faces them and sings or says

	The Lord be with you.
People	And also with you.
Celebrant	Lift up your hearts.
People	We lift them to the Lord.
Celebrant	Let us give thanks to the Lord our God.
People	It is right to give our thanks and praise.

Then, facing the Holy Table, the Celebrant proceeds

We praise you and we bless you, O holy and living God, Creator of heaven and earth.

One of the following proper prefaces is then sung or said

1. Of the First Person of the Trinity

For you create all things that are, that have been, and that will be, made ever new and wondrous in your love.

2. Of the Second Person of the Trinity

For you loved the world so much that you gave your Only-begotten, to take on human flesh and live among us: Jesus the Christ, our Savior.

3. Of the Third Person of the Trinity

For you breathed life into us and filled us with your Holy Spirit, our guardian and guide to fullness of life in Christ.

The celebrant then continues

Therefore we join in the chorus of praise that rings through eternity, with angels and archangels, prophets and martyrs, and all the holy men and women loved by you who have entered into joy. Together with them, we magnify you as we sing (say):

Holy, holy, holy God of power and might.
Heaven and earth are full of your glory.
    Hosanna in the highest.
Blessed is the one who comes in the name of our God.
    Hosanna in the highest.

Then the Celebrant continues

O God, from before time you made ready the creation. Through your Wisdom, your Spirit moved over the deep and brought to birth the heavens: sun, moon, and stars; earth, winds, and waters; growing things, both plants and animals; and finally humankind. You made us in your image, male and female, to love and care for the earth and its creatures as you love and care for us, your children.

You graced us with freedom of heart and mind, but we were heedless and willful. You took us by the hand, and taught us to walk in your ways. And though you led us with cords of compassion and bands of love, we wandered far away. Yet as a mother cares for her children, you would not forget us. Time and again you called us to live in the fullness of your love.

Then you acted anew in Creation. In order that we might see and know the riches of your grace, your Spirit entered into Mary, the maiden of Nazareth, that she might conceive and bear a Son, the holy child of God.

From Advent through the Day of Pentecost, the Celebrant continues according to the season

Advent: The world had waited long in pain and hope, and at last our Savior came to birth, fulfilling the promise of the reign of God in love.

Christmas: Jesus, from his humble and lowly birth, grew in wisdom and stature as the apple of your eye.

Epiphany: He came among us, that your holy light might shine in all the nations of the world.

Baptism: He came to the River Jordan, to be baptized by his cousin John, showing us the way to second birth into holiness and new life.

Lent: He came among us as one knowing weakness and temptation, yet did not sin.

Easter: He came among us, suffered and died, and rising to new life, opened the way into the New Creation.

Ascension: He ascended into heaven to fill all things, and to prepare a place for us.

Pentecost: When he had been raised from the dead, he filled us with the Spirit, your divine breath and fire, the wellspring of zeal, to live the gospel life.

The Celebrant continues

Living among us, Jesus loved us. He yearned to draw all the world to himself, as a hen gathers her young under her wings, yet we would not. We were heedless of his call to walk in love.

At the following words concerning the bread, the Celebrant is to hold it, or lay a hand upon it, and at the words concerning the cup, to hold or place a hand upon the cup and any other vessel containing wine to the consecrated.

At last the time came for him to make the sacrifice of himself, and to be glorified by you. On the night before he died, Jesus was at table with his friends. He took bread, gave thanks to you, broke it, and gave it to them, saying: "Take, eat: This is my Body, which is given for you. Do this for the remembrance of me."

After supper, Jesus took the cup of wine. Again he gave thanks to you, and gave it to them, saying: "Drink this, all of you: This is my Blood of the new Covenant, poured out for you and for all for the forgiveness of sins. Whenever you drink it, do this for the remembrance of me."

As we gather to share the bread and the cup, we remember this loving gift to us:

Celebrant and People

We remember his death on the cross,
We proclaim the resurrection to new life,
We await the return of Christ in glory;

The Celebrant continues

And we join together in the love of Christ to give thanks and praise to you, our God. Here at this table we offer to you all that you have made: this bread and this cup, our (money and) time, and ourselves, a living sacrifice.

Pour out your love and your blessing on all we offer here. Breathe your Spirit into these gifts of bread and wine, to make of them the Body and Blood of Christ. Let your Spirit who broods over the whole creation dwell within us. Gather us to be your holy people, the Body of Christ given for the world you have made. Draw us, O God, to your heart at the heart of the world.

Through Christ and with Christ and in Christ, to whom, with you and the Holy Spirit, be honor and glory, now and for ever. *AMEN.*

As our Savior Christ has taught us, we now pray,

People and Celebrant

Our Father in heaven,
    hallowed be your Name,
    your kingdom come,
    your will be done,
        on earth as in heaven.
Give us today our daily bread.
Forgive us our sins
    as we forgive those who sin against us.

Save us from the time of trial,
    and deliver us from evil.
For the kingdom, the power, and the glory are yours,
    now and for ever. Amen.

The Breaking of the Bread

The Celebrant breaks the consecrated Bread.

A period of silence is kept.

Then may be sung or said

We are the body of Christ:
the broken body and the blood poured out.
We behold who we are;
may we become one with the One we receive.

    or

We are one bread, one body.
We will love one another as Christ loves us.

In place of, or in addition to, the preceding, some other suitable anthem may be used.

Facing the people, the Celebrant says the following Invitation

The Gifts of God for the People of God.

    and may add   Take them in remembrance that Christ died for you, and feed on him in your hearts by faith, with thanksgiving.

The ministers receive the Sacrament in both kinds, and then immediately deliver it to the people.

The Bread and the Cup are given to the communicants with these words

The Body of Christ, the bread of heaven. [*Amen.*]
The Blood of Christ, the cup of salvation. [*Amen.*]

During the ministration of Communion, hymns, psalms, or anthems may be sung.

When necessary, the Celebrant consecrates additional bread and wine, using the form on page 57.

After Communion, the Celebrant says

Let us pray.

For use with First Supplemental Eucharistic Prayer

Celebrant and People

Creator of all,
you have restored us in your image
through Jesus our Savior,
and you have united us in the Sacrament
of Christ's Body and Blood.
Sustain us in our lives of service
as a holy and consecrated body,
through Christ, our life and our joy. Amen.

or

For use with Second Supplemental Eucharistic Prayer

Celebrant and People

Holy, gracious, and loving God,
you have drawn us to your heart,
and nourished us at your table
with holy food and drink,
the Body and Blood of Christ.
Now send us forth

to be your people in the world,
and to proclaim your truth,
this day and evermore. Amen.

The Bishop when present, or the Priest, may bless the people.

The Deacon, or the Celebrant, dismisses them with these words

	Let us go forth in the name of Christ.
People	Thanks be to God.

or this

Deacon	Let us go forth into the world, rejoicing in the power of the Spirit.
People	Thanks be to God.

or this

Deacon	Let us bless the Lord.
People	Thanks be to God.

From the Easter Vigil through the Day of Pentecost "Alleluia, alleluia" may be added to either of the dismissals.

The People respond   Thanks be to God. Alleluia, alleluia.

The Prayers of the People

Any of the forms which follow or those found on pages 383-393 of the Book of Common Prayer may be used.

A bar in the margin indicates petitions which may be omitted.

The particular prayers of the community may be inserted wherever a line in brackets appears.

Prayers of the People—First Supplement

Suggested for use with First Supplemental Eucharistic Prayer

Deacon or other leader

Beloved God, we thank you for giving us power through your Spirit to reveal your life to the world: strengthen, bless, and guide us to make you known by word and example. [_____.]

We are your Church, O God.
Guide us in your grace.

We thank you for your creation, and pray for the earth you have given us to cherish and protect: nourish in us your love for all you have made. [_____.]

We are your stewards, O God.
Guide us in your grace.

Guide and bless us in our work and in our play, and shape the patterns of our political and economic life, that all people may share in the fulfillment of your creative work. [_____.]

We are your servants, O God.
Guide us in your grace.

Awaken our hearts to your presence in all people; in those we love easily and those with whom we struggle, in those different from us and those familiar to us. [_____.]

We are made in your image, O God.
Guide us in your grace.

We thank you for calling us to a glorious heritage as your holy people. Free us from lack of vision, from inertia of will and spirit. By your life-giving Spirit, lead us out of isolation and oppression, redeem and restore us. [_____.]

You are the life within us, O God.
Guide us in your grace.

We thank you for the gift of life, with all its blessings and sorrows. Shield the joyous, comfort and strengthen those in any need or trouble. [_____.] Bless those who will be born today and those who will die, that joining with the company of all your saints we may rejoice in one unending song of praise.

In you alone we have eternal life, O God.
Guide us in your grace.

Celebrant

We offer these our prayers and thanksgivings to you, O God, the source of all that is true and holy, now and for ever. *Amen.*

Prayers of the People–Second Supplement

Suggested for use with Second Supplemental Eucharistic Prayer

Deacon or other leader

In trust, we bring before God our hopes and fears, our wonder and confusion, our joys and sorrows, asking God's blessing on our lives and the life of the world.

Let us pray. *(Silence)*

We pray for the Church, the family of Christ throughout the world, remembering particularly all the baptized who minister in this congregation and community. [Especially _____.]

(Silence)

For the household of faith we pray:
Be with us and bless us, O God.

We pray for our nation. Endow us with your grace, and bring us to a more perfect union embracing young and old, rich and poor, men, women, and children, of all colors and cultures and tongues. [_____.]

   (Silence)

For our nation we pray:
Be with us and guide us, O God.

We pray for all nations, peoples, and tribes throughout the world. In your compassion lead us into the way of unity and peace, and bring us to that glorious liberty which is the birthright of all your children. [_____.]

   (Silence)

For the welfare of the world we pray:
Be with us and unite us, O God.

We pray for our neighbors in this community: at work, at school, and at play. Help us to be aware of those who are unemployed and without shelter, and give us compassion and determination to respond to their needs. [_____.]

   (Silence)

For our community we pray:
Be with us and help us, O God.

We pray for everyone whose body aches, whose heart is weary or frightened, whose mind is confused or cast down. Strengthen with your healing Spirit all who suffer. [Especially _____.] Give us grace to be instruments of your peace.

   (Silence)

For all who suffer and struggle we pray:
Be with us and heal us, O God.

We pray for all those who have died [especially _____]. Draw them to your bosom in love and to the new life of eternity, with [_____ and] all your saints, who have shown us how to live more fully the life of Christ.

   (Silence)

For all who have entered new life in Christ's resurrection we pray:
Be with us and raise us, O God.

Celebrant

O God, who brought all things to birth in creation and gave us grace to become your daughters and sons: Draw us together that we may live in the Spirit as the family of Christ, to ages of ages. *Amen.*

Additional Directions

The Holy Table is spread with a clean white cloth during the celebration.

When the Great Litany is sung or said immediately before the Eucharist, the Litany concludes with the Kyries, and the Eucharist begins with the Salutation and the Collect of the Day. The Prayers of the People following the Creed may be omitted.

The hymn "Splendor and honor," or the hymn used in place of it, is sung or said from Christmas Day through the Feast of the Epiphany; on Sundays from Easter Day through the Day of Pentecost, on all the days of Easter Week, and on Ascension Day; and at other times as desired; but it is not used on the Sundays or ordinary weekdays of Advent or Lent.

The Trisagion, "Holy God," may be sung or said three times, or antiphonally.

The Sanctus found on page 362 of the Book of Common Prayer may be used in place of the Sanctus found in this rite.

The Additional Directions continue with those concerning the Lessons, and all that follows on pages 406–409 of the Prayer Book, except for the following:

Form for Consecrating Additional Elements

Hear us, most merciful God, and with your Word and Holy Spirit bless and sanctify this bread (wine) that it, also, may be the Sacrament of the precious Body (Blood) of Christ, who took bread (the cup) and said, "This is my Body (Blood)." *Amen.*

Musical Supplement

Prepared by the
Standing Commission on Church Music
Daily Morning Prayer: Rite Two Adapted

V. We are the body of Christ: the broken body

and the blood poured out.

R. We be-hold who we are; may we become one

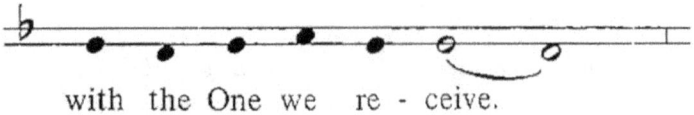

with the One we re-ceive.

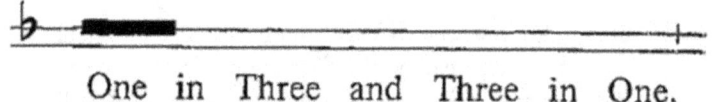

One in Three and Three in One,

for ever and ever. A - men.

Except in Lent, add:

Al - le - lu - ia.

The Antiphons for use with the Venite/Psalm 95 and the Jubilate may be set to music following the models in The Hymnal 1982 at S 294.

Settings for the Venite/Psalm 95 (S 34—S 40) from The Hymnal 1982 can be used with the substitution of "God's" for "his" in the last line. Settings of the Jubilate (S 41—S 45) and the Pascha nostrum (S 46—S 50) require no changes.

The alternative Morning Psalm may be sung to Plainsong or Anglican Chant according to the pointings below. If antiphons are desired for use with this psalm during Advent, Lent, or Easter, one of the appointed opening sentences for the season may be sung as an antiphon.

Psalm 63
Plainsong:

1 O *God*, you are my God; eagerly I séek you; *
† my soul thirsts for you, my flesh faints for you,
    as in a barren and dry land where there is / no wáter.
2 Therefore I have gazed upon you in your hóly place, *
    that I might behold your power and / your glóry.
3 For your loving-kindness is better than lífe itself; *
    my lips / shall gíve you praise.
4 So will I bless you as long as I líve *
    and lift up my hands / in yóur Name.
5 My soul is content, as with marrow and fátness, *
    and my mouth praises you / with jóyful lips,
6 When I remember you upón my bed,
    and meditate on you in the / night wátches.
7 For you have been my hélper, *
    and under the shadow of your wings / I wíll rejoice.
8 My soul clings to you; *
    your right / hand hólds me fast.

Anglican Chant:

1   O God, you are my God;' eagerly I'seek you; *
    my soul thirsts for you, my flesh faints for you,
    as in a barren and dry'land where there'is
    no'water.

2   Therefore I have gazed upon you in your'holy'place, *
    that I might be'hold your'power and your'glory.

3 For your loving-kindness is better than ' life it ' self; *
    my ' lips shall ' give you ' praise.

4 So will I bless you as ' long as I ' live *
    and lift ' up my ' hands in your ' Name.

5 My soul is content, as with ' marrow and ' fatness, *
    and my mouth ' praises you with ' joyful ' lips,

6 When I remember you up ' on my ' bed, *
    and ' meditate on ' you in the ' night watches.

7 For you have ' been my ' helper, *
    and under the shadow of your ' wings I ' will
    re ' joice.

8 My ' söul ' clings to you; *
    your ' right hand ' holds me ' fast.

Morning Prayer Canticles

9A *The First Song of Isaiah*

Surely, it is ' God who ' saves me; *
I will ' trust and will ' not be a ' fraid.

The remaining verses as in The Hymnal 1982.

12A *A Song of Creation*

One or more sections of this Canticle may be used. Whatever the selection, it begins with the Invocation and concludes with the Doxology.

Invocation

1 Glorify the Lord, all you ' works of the ' Lord, *
    sing ' praise and give ' honor for ' ever.
2 In the high vault of heaven, ' glorify the ' Lord, *
    sing ' praise and give ' honor for ' ever.

I The Cosmic Order

3 Glorify the Lord, you angels and all ' powers
        of the ' Lord, *
    O heavens and all ' waters a ' bove the ' heavens.
4 Sun and moon and stars of the sky, ' glorify the ' Lord, *
    sing ' praise and give ' honor for ' ever.
5 Glorify the Lord, every shower of ' rain and fall of ' dew. *
    all ' winds and ' fire and ' heat.
6 Winter and summer, ' glorify the ' Lord, *
    sing ' praise and give ' honor for ' ever.
7 Glorify the Lord, O ' chill and ' cold, *
    drops of ' dew and ' flakes of ' snow.
8 Frost and cold, ice and sleet, ' glorify the ' Lord, *
    sing ' praise and give ' honor for ' ever.
9 Glorify the Lord, O ' nights and ' days, *
    O shining ' light and en ' folding ' dark.
10 Storm clouds and thunderbolts, ' glorify the ' Lord, *
    sing ' praise and give ' honor for ' ever.

II The Earth and its Creatures

11 Let the earth glorify the Lord, *
    sing praise and give honor for ever.
12 Glorify the Lord, O mountains and hills,
    and all that grows upon the earth, *
    sing praise and give honor for ever.
13 Glorify the Lord, O springs of water, seas, and streams, *
    O whales and all that move in the waters.
14 All birds of the air, glorify the Lord, *
    sing praise and give honor for ever.
15 Glorify the Lord, O beasts of the wild, *
    and all you flocks and herds.
16 O men and women everywhere, glorify the Lord, *
    sing praise and give honor for ever.

III The People of God

17 Let the people of God glorify the Lord, *
    sing praise and give honor for ever.
18 Glorify the Lord, O priests and servants
       of the Lord, *
    sing praise and give honor for ever.

19 Glorify the Lord, O spirits and ' souls of
    the ' righteous, *
    sing ' praise and give ' honor for ' ever.
20 You that are holy and humble of heart, ' glorify the ' Lord, *
    sing ' praise and give ' honor for ' ever.

Doxology
21 Let us glorify the Lord: Father, Son, and ' Holy ' Spirit: *
    sing ' praise and give ' honor for ' ever.
22 In the high vault of heaven, ' glorify the ' Lord, *
    sing ' praise and give ' honor for ' ever.

13A *A Song of Praise*

> The settings (S 231–S 236) in The Hymnal 1982 may be used by substituting "forebears" for "fathers" in the first line.

14A *A Song of Penitence*

> The small textual changes in verses 5 and 8 of this Canticle do not affect its Anglican Chant settings in The Hymnal 1982 (S 238–S 241).

15A *The Song of Mary*

1 My soul proclaims the greatness of the Lord,
    my spirit rejoices in ' God my ' Savior; *
        for you, Lord, have looked with ' favor
        on your ' lowly ' servant.

2 From this day all generations will ˈcall me ˈblessèd: *
   you, the Almighty, have done great things for me,
   and ˈholy ˈis your ˈName.
3 You have mercy on ˈthose who ˈfear you *
   from generˈation to ˈgenerˈation.
4 You have shown ˈstrength with your ˈarm *
   and scattered the ˈproud in ˈtheir conˈceit,
5 casting down the ˈmighty from their ˈthrones *
   and ˈlifting ˈup the ˈlowly.
6 You have filled the ˈhungry with ˈgood things *
   and ˈsent the ˈrich away ˈempty.
7 You have come to the aid of your ˈservant ˈIsrael, *
   to reˈmember the ˈpromise of ˈmercy,
8 The promise ˈmade to our ˈforebears, *
   to ˈAbraham and his ˈchildren for ˈever.

16A *The Song of Zechariah*

1 Blessèd are you, Lord, the ˈGod of ˈIsrael, *
   you have come to your ˈpeople and ˈset
   them ˈfree.
2 You have raised up for us a ˈmighty ˈSavior, *
   born of the ˈhouse of your ˈservant ˈDavid.
3 Through your holy prophets you promised of old
   to ˈsave us from our ˈenemies, *
   from the ˈhands of ˈall who ˈhate us.

4 To show ʹmercy to ourʹforebears, *
   and to reʹmember yourʹholyʹcovenant.
5 This was the oath you swore to ourʹfatherʹAbraham: *
   to set usʹfree from theʹhands of ourʹenemies,
6 Free to worship you withʹoutʹfear, *
   holy and righteous beʹfore you all theʹdays of
   ourʹlife.
7 And you, child, shall be called the prophet of
   theʹMostʹHigh. *
   for you will go before theʹLord to preʹpare theʹway,
8 To give God's peopleʹknowledge of salʹvation *
   by the forʹgivenessʹof theirʹsins.
9 In the tender comʹpassion of ourʹGod *
   the dawn from onʹhigh shallʹbreak upʹon us,
10 To shine on those who dwell in darkness and
   theʹshadow ofʹdeath, *
   and to guide ourʹfeet into theʹway ofʹpeace.

18A *A Song to the Lamb*

1 Splendor and honor andʹroyalʹpower *
   are yours byʹright, OʹGod MostʹHigh,
2 For you createdʹeverything thatʹis, *
   and by your will they were creʹated andʹhave theirʹbeing.
3 And yours by right, OʹLamb that wasʹslain, *
   for with yourʹblood you have reʹdeemed forʹGod,

4 From every family, language,ˈpeople, andˈnation, *
   a royalˈpriesthood toˈserve ourˈGod.

5 And so, to the One whoˈsits upon theˈthrone, *
   —ˈand toˈChrist theˈLamb,

6 Be worship and praise, doˈminion andˈsplendor, *
   forˈever and forˈeverˈmore.

20A Glory to God

By substituting "God's people" for "his people" in the first sentence, the settings (S 272—S 281) in The Hymnal 1982 can be used for this Canticle.

21A You are God

1 We praise you, O God,
   we acˈclaim you asˈLord; *
     all creation worships you,
     theˈFatherˈeverˈlasting.
2 To you all angels, all theˈpowers ofˈheaven, *
     the cherubim and seraphim,ˈsing inˈendlessˈpraise:
3 Holy holy, holy Lord, God ofˈpower andˈmight, *
     heaven andˈearth areˈfull of yourˈglory.
4 The glorious company of aˈpostlesˈpraise you. *
     The nobleˈfellowship ofˈprophetsˈpraise you.
5 The white-robed army ofˈmartyrsˈpraise you. *
     Throughout the world theˈholyˈChurch acˈclaims you:

6 Father, of ˈmajesty unˈbounded, *
   your true and only Son, ˈworthy ofˈallˈworship,
§7 theˈHolyˈSpirit, *
   —ˈadvoˈcate andˈguide.

8 You, Christ, are theˈking ofˈglory, *
   the eˈternalˈSon of theˈFather.
9 When you took our flesh toˈset usˈfree *
   you humblyˈchose theˈVirgin'sˈwomb.
10 You overcame theˈsting ofˈdeath *
   and opened the kingdom ofˈheaven toˈall beˈlievers.
11 You are seated at God'sˈright hand inˈglory. *
   We believe that you willˈcome toˈbe ourˈjudge.
12 Come then, Lord, andˈhelp yourˈpeople, *
   bought with theˈprice ofˈyour ownˈblood,
13 and bring usˈwith yourˈsaints *
   toˈgloryˈeverˈlasting.

§ *Second half of a double chant.*

22 A Song of Wisdom

1 Wisdom freed from aˈnation of opˈpressors *
   a holyˈpeople and aˈblamelessˈrace.
2 She entered the soul of aˈservant of theˈLord, *
   withstood dreadˈrulers withˈwonders andˈsigns.

3 To the saints she gave the re′ward of their′labors, *
   and′led them by a′marvelous′way;
4 She was their′shelter by′day *
   and a′blaze of′stars by′night.

5 She brought them across the′Rëd′Sea, *
   she′led them through′mighty′waters;
6 But their enemies she′swallowed in the′waves *
   and spewed them′out from the′depths of the a′byss.

7 And then, Lord, the righteous sang′hymns to your′Name, *
   and praised with one′voice your pro′tecting′hand;
8 For Wisdom opened the′mouths of the′mute, *
   and gave speech to the′tongues of a′new-born′people.

23 *A Song of Pilgrimage*

1 Before I ventured forth,
   even while I was′very′young, *
   I sought wisdom′openly′in my′prayer.
2 In the forecourts of the temple I′asked for′her, *
   and I will′seek her′to the′end.
3 From first blossom to′early′fruit. *
   she has′been the de′light of my′heart.
4 My foot has kept firmly to the′true′path, *
   diligently from my′youth have′I pur′sued her.

§ 5 I inclined my ear a ˈlittle and reˈceived her; *
   I found for myself much ˈwisdom and beˈcame
   a ˈdept in her.
 6 To the One who gives me wisdom ˈwill I give ˈglory, *
   for I have resolved to ˈlive acˈcording to her ˈway.
 7 I have been ˈzealous for the ˈgood, *
   in order that I ˈmight not be ˈput to ˈshame.
 8 My soul has ˈbeen subdued by ˈher, *
   and I have been ˈcareful ˈin my ˈconduct.
 9 I spread out my ˈhands to the ˈheavens, *
   and laˈmented my ˈignorance ˈof her.
10 I directed my ˈsoul to ˈher, *
   and through purifiˈcation ˈhave Iˈfound her.
11 From the beginning I gained ˈcourage ˈfrom her, *
   therefore I ˈwill not ˈbe for ˈsaken.
12 In my inmost being have I been ˈstirred to ˈseek her, *
   therefore have I ˈgained a ˈgood pos ˈsession.
13 As my reward the Almighty has given me the ˈgift
   of ˈlanguage, *
   and with it will I ˈoffer ˈpraise to ˈGod.

§ *Second half of a double chant.*

The Prayers

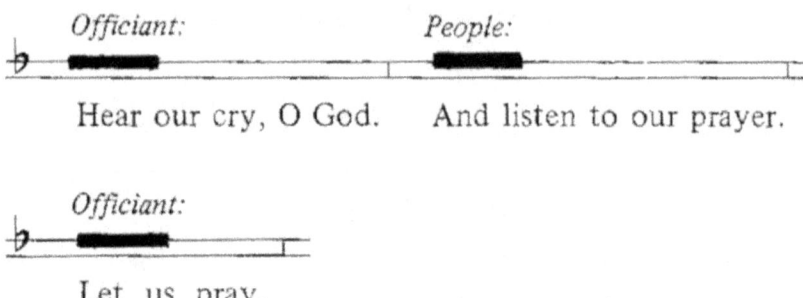

Officiant: Hear our cry, O God.   People: And listen to our prayer.

Officiant: Let us pray.

The Tone for the Salutation and the Lord's Prayer can be found in The Hymnal 1982 at S 51.

Suffrages A will be found at S 52 in The Hymnal 1982

Suffrages B

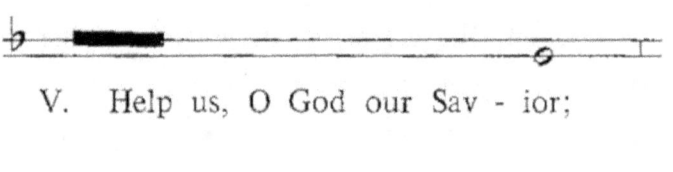

V. Help us, O God our Sav - ior;

R. Deliver us and forgive us our sins.

V. Look upon your congrega - tion;

Supplemental Liturgical Texts 71

R. Give to your people the bless-ing of peace.

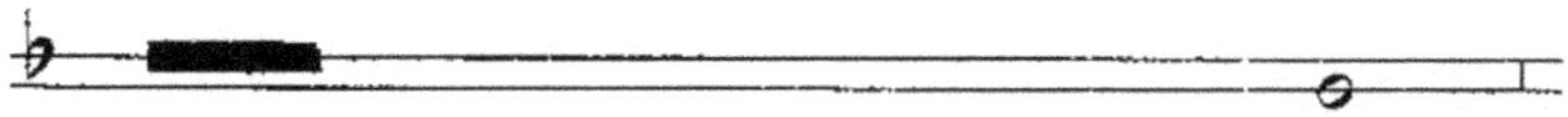

V. Declare your glory among the na - tions.

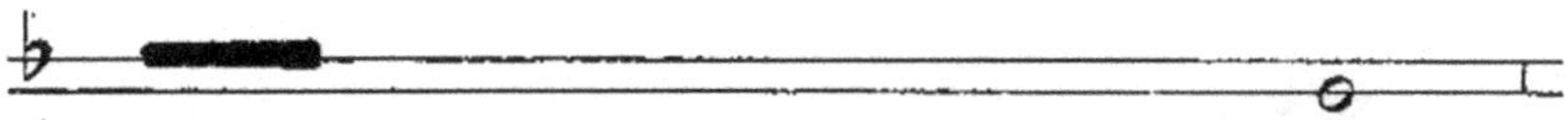

R. And your wonders among all peo - ples.

V. Let not the oppressed be shamed

and turned a - way.

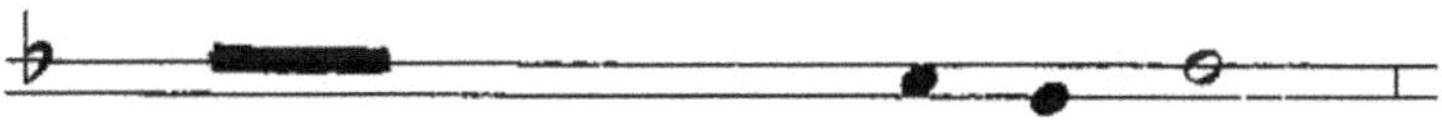

R. Never forget the lives of your poor.

V. Continue your loving-kindness to

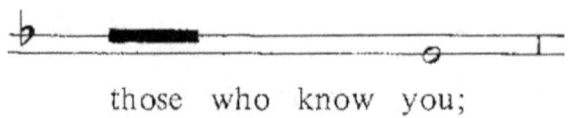
those who know you;

R. And your favor to those who are true of heart.

V. Satisfy us by your loving-kindness

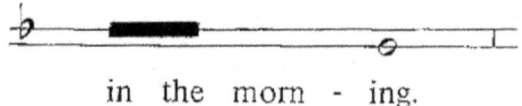
in the morn - ing.

R. So shall we rejoice and be glad

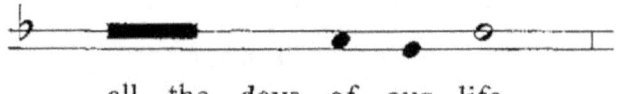
all the days of our life.

Supplemental Liturgical Texts 73

Suffrages C

Cantor or Officiant:
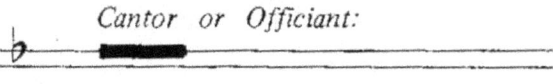
V. Save your people, Lord, and

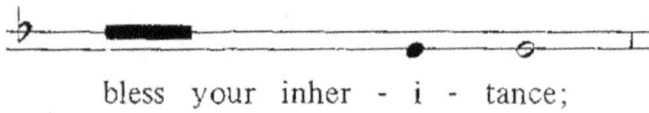
bless your inher - i - tance;

People:

R. Govern and uphold them, now and al - ways.

V. Day by day we bless you;

R. We praise your Name for ev - er.

V. Keep us today, Lord, from all sin.

74 PRAYER BOOK STUDIES 30

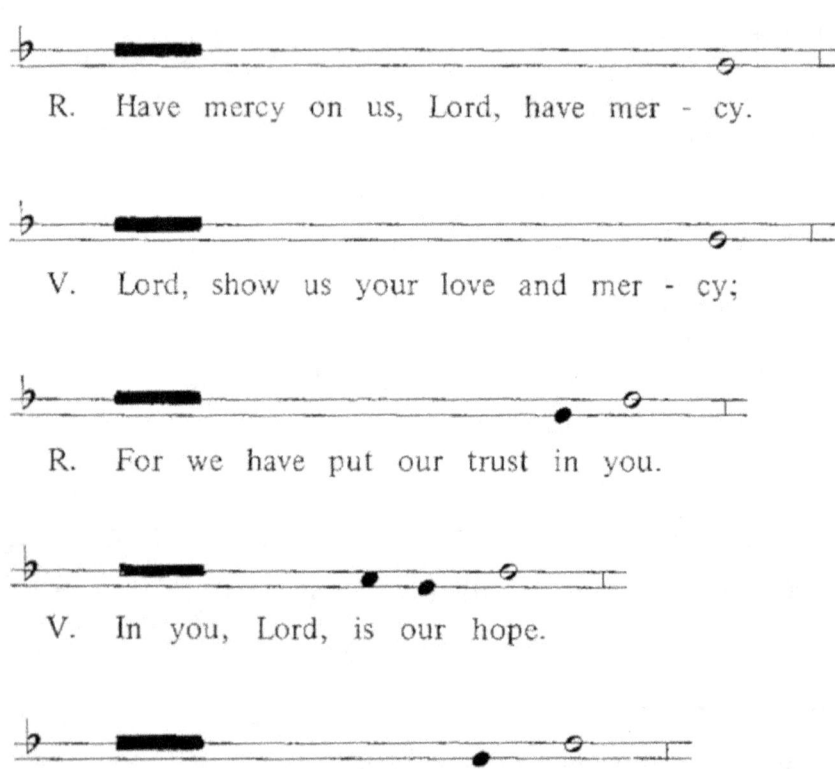

R. Have mercy on us, Lord, have mercy.

V. Lord, show us your love and mercy;

R. For we have put our trust in you.

V. In you, Lord, is our hope.

R. Let us never be put to shame.

Settings for Collect Tone II (S 448) and for the Concluding Versicle and Response (S54—S55) will be found in The Hymnal 1982.

An Order of Worship for the Evening *Adapted*

Settings for the first Greeting will be found at S 56 and S 57 in The Hymnal 1982.

From Easter Day through the Day of Pentecost.

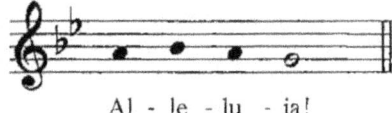

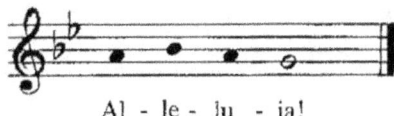

Music: *O filii et filiae*, adapt. SCCM

Or this:

Music: *Victimae Paschali laudes*, adapt. SCCM

Music: *Victimae Paschali laudes*, adapt. SCCM

In Lent and other penitential occasions:

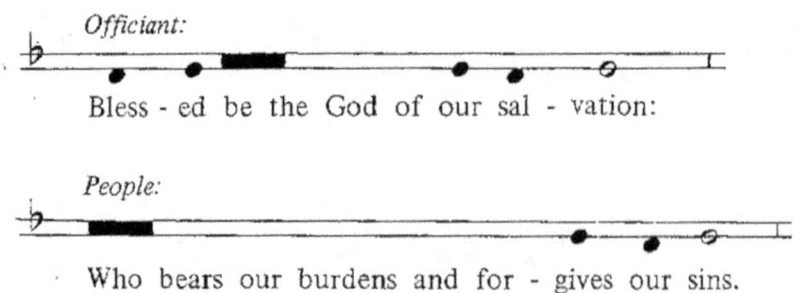

A Tone for the Short Lesson will be found at S 449 in The Hymnal 1982. The Collect Tones are at S 447 and S 448.

Settings of the Phos hilaron can be found at S 59—S 61 in The Hymnal 1982.

Psalm 134

Plainsong:

Behöld now, bless the Lord, all you sérvants óf the Lord, *
 you that stand by night in the/house of túë Lord.
Lift up your hands in the holy pláce and bléss the Lord; *
 the Lord who made heaven and earth bless you/out of Źion.

Anglican Chant:

Behold now, bless the Lord, all you ' servants of the ' Lord, *
you that stand by ' night in the ' house of the ' Lord.

Lift up your hands in the holy place and ' bless the ' Lord; *
the Lord who made heaven and earth ' bless you ' out of ' Zion.

Psalm 141:1-3, 8ab

Plainsong:

O Lord, I call to you; come to me quíckly; *
 hear my voice/when I crý to you.
Let my prayer be set forth in your sight as íncense, *
 the lifting up of my hands as the/evening sácrifice.
Set a watch before my mouth, O Lord, and guard the door of my líps; *
 let not my heart incline to/any évil thing.
My eyes are turned to yóu, Lord God; *
 in/you I táke refuge.

Anglican Chant:

O Lord, I call to you;ˈcome to meˈquickly; *
hear myˈvoiceˈwhen Iˈcry to you.

Let my prayer be set forth in yourˈsight asˈincense, *
the lifting up of myˈhands as theˈeveningˈsacrifice.

Set a watch before my mouth, O Lord,
and guard theˈdoor of myˈlips; *
let not my heart incline toˈanyˈevilˈthing.

My eyes are turned toˈyou, LordˈGod; *
inˈyou Iˈtakeˈrefuge.

> *Tones for the Aaronic Blessing will be found in the Musical Appendix of the Altar Book, which also contains the Tone for Blessings.*
>
> *Tones for Dismissals (S 174—S 176) are in The Hymnal 1982.*

Daily Evening Prayer: Rite Two Adapted

Preces

> *The alternative Preces will be found at S 58 in The Hymnal 1982; the alternative to the Gloria Patri will be found in the settings for Daily Morning Prayer: Rite Two Adapted (p. 84). For the Phos hilaron or alternative Psalms see The Order of Worship for Evening Adapted (p. 102).*
>
> *The pointing of the Magnificat for Anglican Chant can be-found at Canticle 15A in Daily Morning Prayer: Rite Two Adapted (p. 90). Settings for the Nunc dimittis (S 253—S 260, S 405) can be found in The Hymnal 1982.*

The Prayers

> *The Versicle and Response before the Lord's Prayer are the same as in Daily Morning Prayer: Rite Two Adapted (p. 97). A Tone for the Salutation will be found in The Hymnal 1982 at S 62.*

For Suffrages A, see S 52 in The Hymnal 1982. Two Tones (S 63—S 64) are also provided there for Suffrages B, which can be used fo the adapted rite by substituting "God" for "Lord" in the People's response.

The Tone for the Collects (S 448) and ones for the concluding Versicle and Response (S 65—S 66) can be found in The Hymnal 1982.

The Holy Eucharist

Opening Acclamation

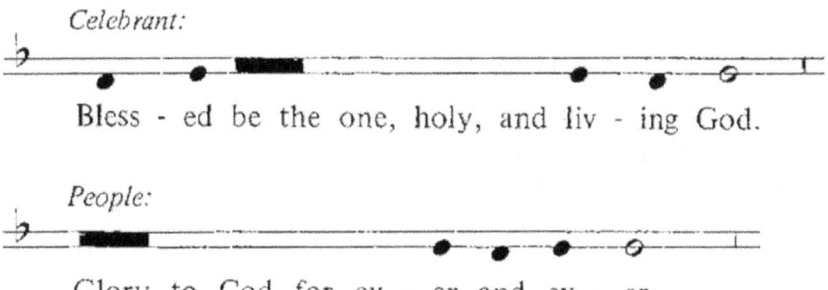

From Easter Day through the Day of Pentecost:

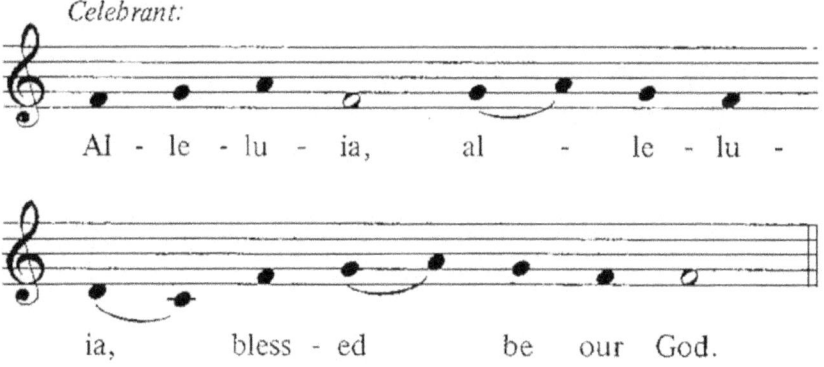

For the Lenten Acclamation, see Order of Worship for Evening, (p. 104)

For the Anglican Chant pointing of the Song of Praise, see Canticle 18A (p. 92). Settings of The Trisagion (S 99–S 102, S 360) will be found in The Hymnal 1982.

The Peace

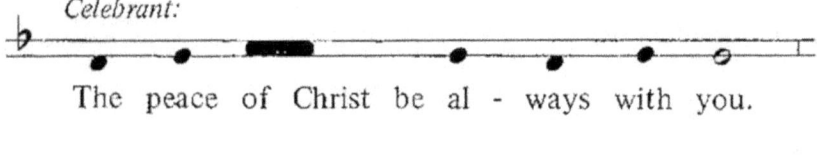

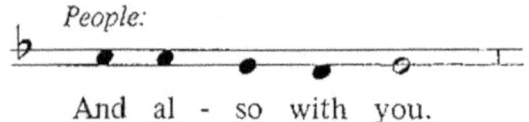

The Sursum cords in the Supplemental Eucharistic Prayers can be sung to S 120 in The Hymnal 1982 by substituting "our" for "him" in the last response of the People.

Supplemental Liturgical Texts 81

The Preface: First Supplemental Eucharistic Prayer

It is good and joyful that in your presence we give you thanks, Holy God.

for you have included us in creation and made us in your glorious image.

You have remembered us from our beginning and fed us with your

The Preface: Second Supplemental Eucharistic Prayer

One of the following proper prefaces is sung:

Supplemental Liturgical Texts 83

Of the First Person of the Trinity

We praise you and we bless you,

O ho-ly and liv-ing God,

Cre-a - tor of heav'n and earth.

For you create all things that are, that have been,

and that will be, made ev-er new

and won-drous in your love.

Of the Second Person of the Trinity

Of the Third Person of the Trinity

We praise you and we bless you,
O ho-ly and liv-ing God, Cre-a-tor of heav'n and earth. For you breathed life in-to us and filled us with your Ho-ly Spir-it, our guard-ian and guide to full-ness of life in Christ.

The Celebrant then continues:

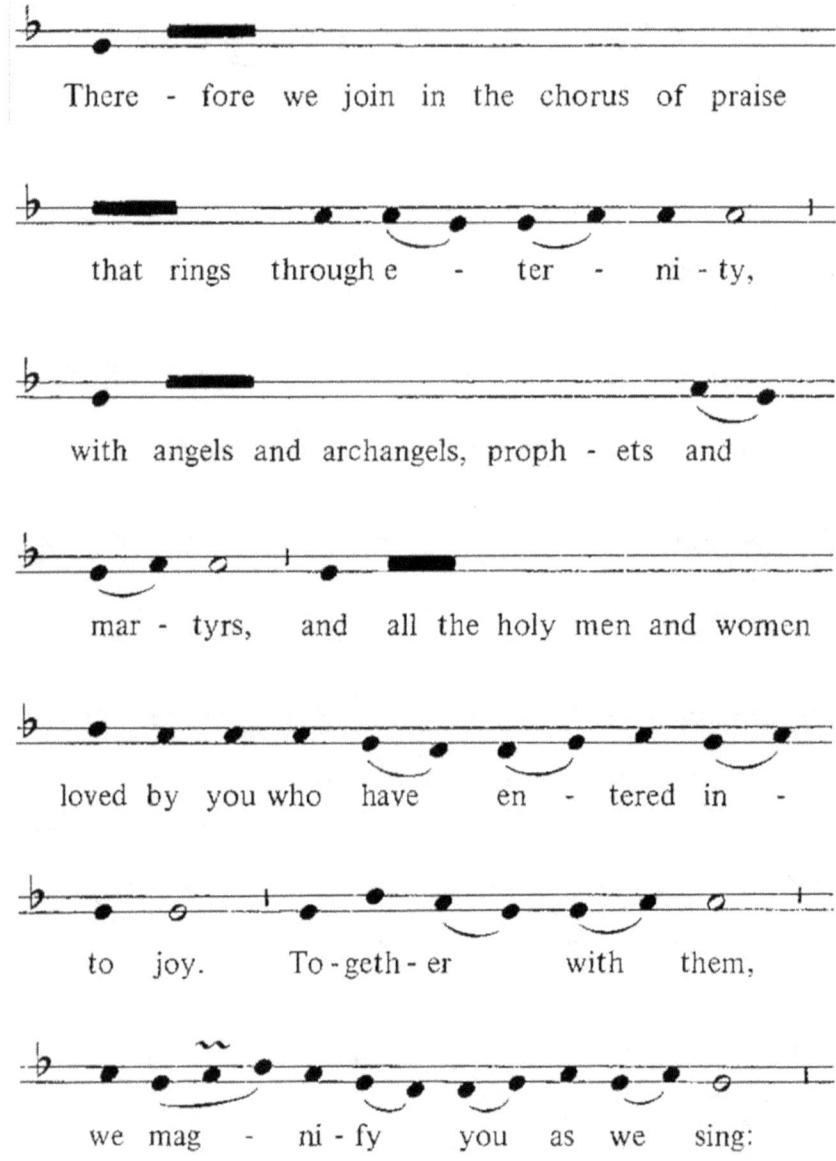

Supplemental Liturgical Texts 87

S 124 Adapted

Ho - ly, ho - ly, ho - ly
God of pow - er and might, heav - en and earth are full of your glo - ry.
Ho - san - na in the high - est.
Bless - ed is the one who comes in the name of our God. Ho - san - na in the high - est.

Setting: from *New Plainsong;* David Hurd (b. 1950), adapt.
Copyright © 1981, G.I.A. Publications, Inc.

S 125 Adapted

Setting: From *A Community Mass*; Richard Proulx (b. 1937), adapt.
Copyright © 1971, 1977, G.I.A. Publications, Inc.

S 128 Adapted

Supplemental Liturgical Texts 91

Setting: William Mathias (b. 1934), adapt.
Copyright © 1976, Oxford University Press, Inc.

S 130 Adapted

Supplemental Liturgical Texts 93

Supplemental Liturgical Texts 95

… in the name of our God. Ho-san-na … in the high-est. Ho -

Setting from *Deutche Messe*, Franz Peter Schubert (1797-1828):
arr. Richard Proulx (b. 1937), adapt.
Adaptation copyright © 1985, G.I.A. Publications, Inc.

Conclusion of the Eucharistic Prayer

First Supplemental Prayer

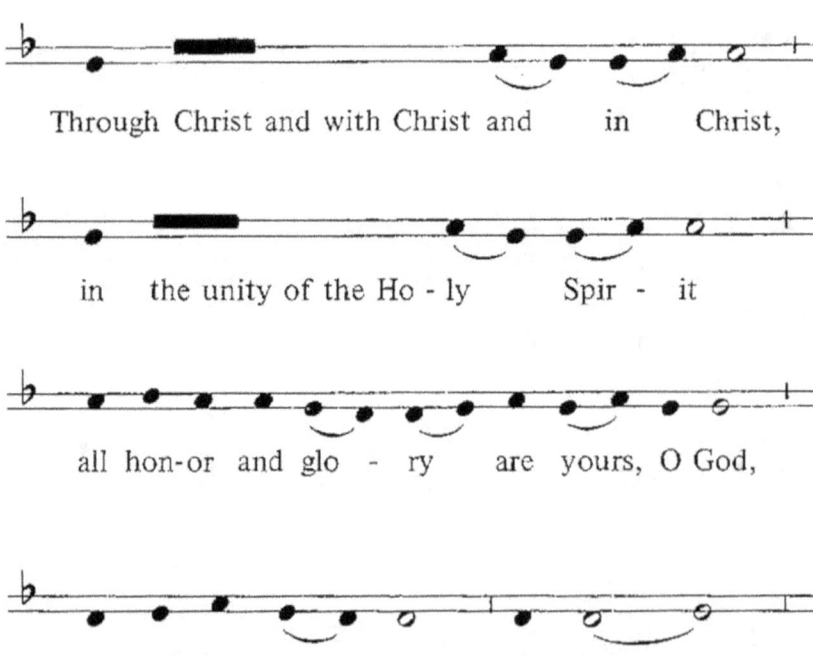

Supplemental Liturgical Texts 97

Second Supplemental Prayer

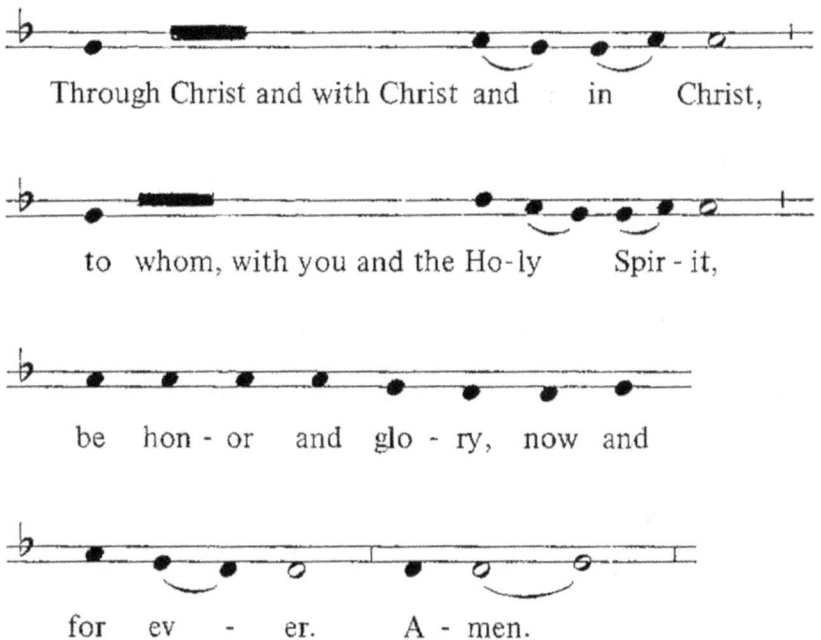

Fraction Anthem

This anthem may be sung in full by all, or by the choir, or as a versicle and response.

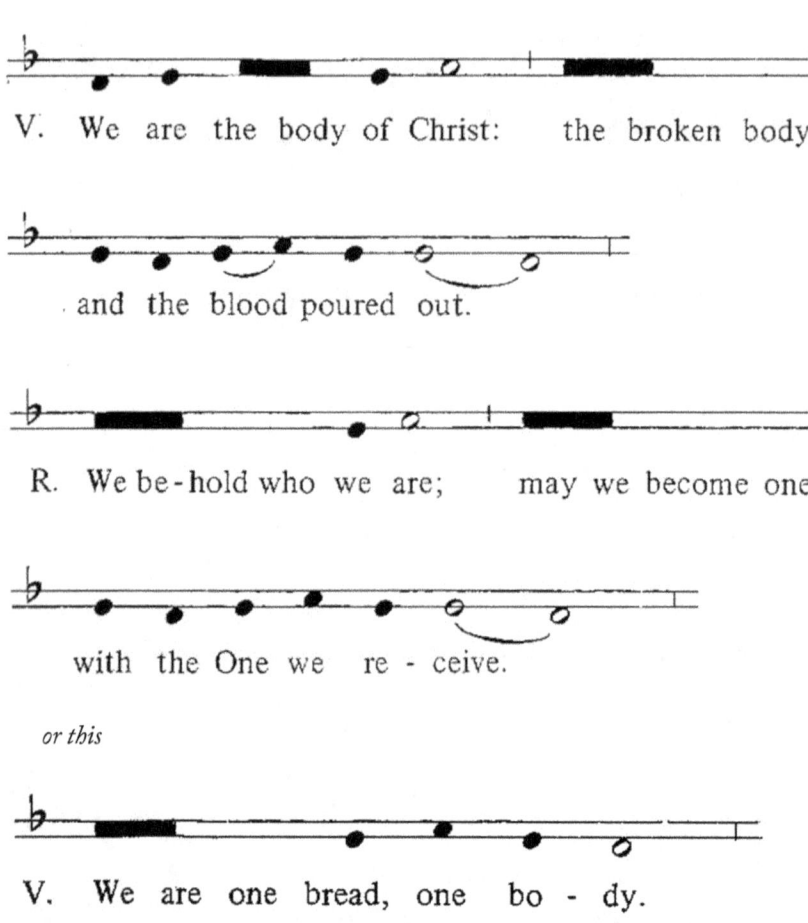

V. We are the body of Christ: the broken body and the blood poured out.

R. We be-hold who we are; may we become one with the One we re-ceive.

or this

V. We are one bread, one bo-dy.

R. We will love one another as Christ loved us.

Tones for the Invitation to Communion and for Blessings can be found in the Musical Appendix of the Altar Book. Tones for Dismissals (S174—S 176) are in The Hymnal 1982.

Prayers of the People: First Form

This form of the Prayers of the People can be sung according to the following formula:

Deacon or Cantor:

Beloved God, . . . We are your Church, O God.
We thank you . . . We are your servants, O God.
Etc.

People:

Guide us in your grace.

The People's response may be sung in parts:

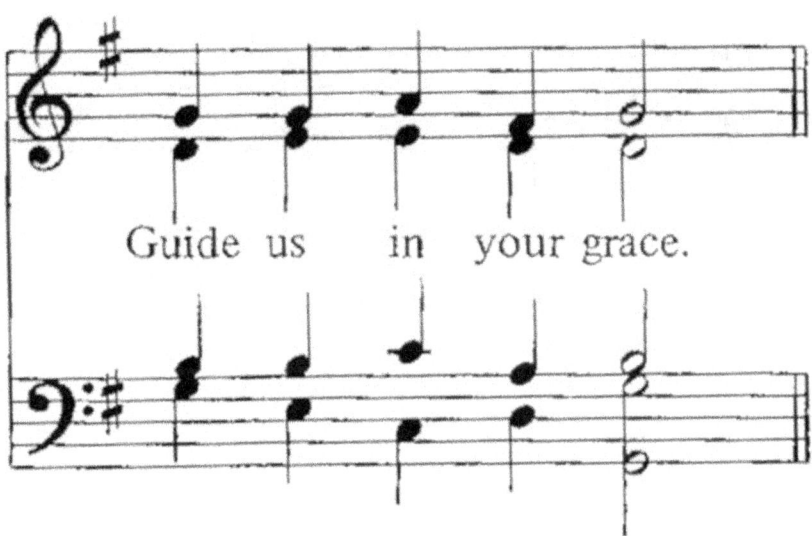

Guide us in your grace.

As may the Amen:

The Celebrant's concluding prayer may be monotoned or sung to Collect Tone II (S 448).

COMMENTARY ON PRAYER BOOK STUDIES 30

Containing
Supplemental Liturgical Materials

1989

Acknowledgments

The translations of the *Gloria Patri, Benedictus Dominus Deus, Magnificat, Te Deum laudamus, Gloria in excelsis,* Apostles' Creed, Lord's Prayer, Suffrages C at Morning Prayer, Nicene Creed, and *Sursum corda* used in this book are those proposed to the churches by the ecumenical English Language Liturgical Commission (ELLC). Copyright © 1987, ELLC. All rights reserved.

Grateful acknowledgment is made of the contribution of those who wrote and edited this Commentary: the Rev. Leonel L. Mitchell; the Rev. Joseph P. Russell; Sr. Jean Campbell, OSH; Mr. Howard E. Galley; the Rev. Sarah H. Motley; and the Rev. Linda S. Strohmier. The Rt. Rev. Vincent King Pettit, chair, the Standing Liturgical Commission; The Rev. Canon Lloyd S. Casson, chair, the Committee on Supplemental Liturgical Texts

1. Background

Leonel L. Mitchell

"The world to which we are sent to proclaim Christ is constantly changing, and the gospel needs to be translated into terms which the world can understand. This means more than translating the actual language of the proclamation . . . It means translating its thought into forms which our culture can comprehend, so that the original message shines through undistorted."[1]

When I wrote those words in 1975, the topic under discussion was the services then undergoing trial use which became the Book of Common Prayer 1979. The situation today is no different. Change is still the only constant factor in our history. At the present moment our concern is ongoing change in the English language and its effect on the way we pray.

Language and Change

Anglicanism for over four centuries has been concerned that people pray in their own language. In the 1970s the Episcopal Church, like most English-speaking churches throughout the world, began to celebrate the liturgy in 20th century English. For 400 years the language of Cranmer and the King James Bible had been determinative for the way in which English-speaking people had framed their prayers. This is no longer true. All across the ecclesiastical spectrum God is regularly addressed in both public and private prayer in contemporary language. Liturgies, whether Anglican, Roman, Lutheran, or Reformed, use formal contemporary speech, and when the Scripture is read, even the Revised Standard Version may sound quaint or antiquated.

One of the characteristics of a living language is that it grows and changes, adding new words to its vocabulary and changing the meanings of existing ones. Words such as "quick" meaning "living" or "prevent" meaning "precede" can no longer be used without their probably being misunderstood. Sometimes words do not change their actual denotation, but gain or lose social acceptability, or positive or negative connotations. They are still understood, but the message they send is distorted. An example of this is the word "stink," which is now always unpleasant and impolite, but which originally referred to any kind of odor.

Changes that have already taken place are one thing, but while change is actually happening, it is more difficult to appreciate and may actually become a source of misunderstanding or heated controversy. Proper names such as the National Association for the Advancement of Colored People and the United Negro College Fund bear witness to the changing ways in which African Americans in this

---

1. Leonel L. Mitchell, *Liturgical Change: How Much Do We Need?* (New York: Seabury Press. 1975) pp. 9f.

century have referred to themselves. Praying in contemporary English, then, may involve us in a continuous updating of our language, not so that we may say new and different things, but so we may continue to say the same thing without our words distorting what we say.

Technical Language and Liturgical Language

Academic theology, by contrast, has generally operated by carefully defining technical terms to insure precision of meaning. All technical disciplines, including nuclear physics, computer programming, and football coaching, tend to operate this way. The words "strike" and "hit," which are synonyms in ordinary English, mean quite different things to a baseball fan. In academic writing, technical terms are frequently imported from another language to avoid being subject to the varieties of meaning on which the living language thrives. We speak of *ecclesia* to escape the ambiguity of "church," or *anamnesis* to avoid "remembrance" or "memorial," and the eucharistic controversies of the sixteenth century which involved those concepts. Scholars may use this language in their private prayers, but the liturgy must speak a language more accessible to all. This language often lacks the precision of technical theological jargon, and, like all natural language, is capable of many levels of understanding and meaning. It may be poetic and imaginative, but it must speak the truth.

Liturgical language is theological language, but it is not the language of academic theology. It is the language of "primary theology," of address to.God. It embodies the images and metaphors in which we think of and speak to our God. This language of prayer and hymn shapes our theological understanding much more surely than articles in theological journals. Anglican theology itself, as much as Anglican piety, has been shaped in this way over the years by the liturgy of the Book of Common Prayer.

Whether in prayer or in academic theology, the language in which we speak of God is necessarily metaphorical, or analogical. We cannot use human words to speak of God in the same sense in which we use them to speak of human beings. Even words like "good" and "powerful" mean something different when applied to God. These words are perhaps the best analogies we can find to the divine attributes, but they are not exact fits.

> For my thoughts are not your thoughts,
>   nor your ways my ways, says the Lord.
> For as the heavens are higher than the earth,
>   so are my ways higher than your ways,
>   and my thoughts than your thoughts.[2]

---

2. Isaiah 55:8-9 (Canticle 10, BCP p. 86)

Any image of God or theological construct we may have is too small, too narrow, and grossly inadequate. Some are more obviously inadequate than others, but when human reason and language have gone as far as they can, there is still further to go and more to comprehend. The Cappadocian Fathers understood this. The great scholastics of the Middle Ages understood this. The Reformers understood it. So did the Caroline divines, and so do contemporary theologians.

Analogous and Literal Language

It is almost impossible for human beings to avoid using anthropomorphic terms in thinking about God, and, even if we are able to avoid such terms in theological discourse, we do not pray to a "prime mover unmoved" or a "first caused uncaused." The more "real" and "personal" our notion of God is, the more anthropomorphic our language is likely to be. As Christians we properly justify the use of such language in terms of the incarnation and the *imago Dei*. Christ is "the image of the invisible God,"[3] and we are all, male and female, made in the divine image.[4]

The great problem of all the figures, images, and metaphors used in the liturgy is that we begin to forget that they are used analogically, and to think of them as literal descriptions. We think of God as wearing a crown, or carrying a shepherd's crook, or seated on a throne. These mental pictures may be devotionally helpful to us, as long as we remember that they are our images, not pictures of God in the reality and fullness of the divine being. The more apt the metaphor, the more likely we are to forget that it is a metaphor. When Jesus says, "I am the vine," we all recognize that it is a figure of speech, but we are apt to forget that "I and the Father are one" is not literal description.

Many of the images of God we use in our worship are biblical. Others have their roots in the theological tradition of the early Church. Some are medieval or modern. All are rooted in human understanding and tend to lose or change their meaning as the cultural matrices in which they are grounded change. Marianne Micks wrote, "Symbols slip. All symbols slip. The symbol breakers who have appeared regularly in the Christian community, smashing other men's efforts to figure forth the One whom they worship, have recognized this."[5] Throughout the centuries liturgies have been subject to this slippage.

In the 16th century a favorite metaphor for God was King. In 1547, the year of Henry VIII's death, a prayer still in the English Prayer Book addressed God as "high and mighty, King of Kings, Lord of Lords, the only ruler of Princes, who dost from thy throne behold all the dwellers upon earth."[6] In Tudor England this

---

3. Colossians 1:15

4. Genesis 1:26

5. Marianne Micks, *The Future Present* (New York: Seabury Press. 1979) p. 159.

6. "A Prayer for the King's Majesty" at the end of Mattins in the 1662 Prayer Book.

image of God as a monarch on a lofty throne with faithful subjects humbly presenting their petitions and supplications was one which emerged naturally out of that context. It evoked the familiar image of a real royal court. The original metaphor of God as "King of Kings" is biblical, but it is fleshed out with the trappings of Tudor monarchy, and from our perspective it seems to suggest arrogance and unapproachability and thereby distorts the image of God.

In the present Prayer Book there has been a move away from royal imagery, not because we no longer believe the truth which is expressed in the metaphor of divine kingship, but because the image is not congenial or immediately available to us. For us, kings and queens bring to mind either symbolic authority with little or no real power, as in most modern constitutional monarchies, tyranny, or a fairy-tale world of make believe. It is not that we cannot remythologize the image into one which we do understand, but that we must run an image like "The Lord is King"[7] through a number of mental filters before it can have the same meaning to us it had to the psalmist. In the 1979 Prayer Book, the text of the psalms was not altered to remove the image, but it is not used in prayers as frequently as in previous Prayer Books, and it is balanced with other images.

Another unquestionably biblical image is "Father." Jesus called God "Father" and taught his disciples to do the same. It is an image of God we do not find often in the Old Testament.[8] It represents a distinctive insight into Jesus' own relationship with God and the relationship into which he calls us, his brothers and sisters, and so is by no means an image which the Church can do entirely without. But if this is the only image we use, we are apt not only to use it correctly — to name the unbegotten Source of Godhead in the other two persons of the Trinity, and to express the intensely personal relationship implied by the word "Abba" on the lips of Jesus — but also incorrectly, to invest the One who is "without body, parts, or passions"[9] with human characteristics like maleness, or a beard, or even the faults of human fathers.

Images to Enrich Liturgical Language

In a theological essay such as this one, we are free to include a footnote to explain more precisely how God is properly addressed as "Father" and of what we must be wary in doing so, just as we can explain that the use of masculine pronouns to refer to One without sex is simply a grammatical convention and does not imply that the antecedent is male. Liturgy does not have this option. The words are spoken in all of their ambiguity and are not always understood in the sense that the

---

7. Psalm 97:1; 99:1

8. It occurs in Psalm 89:26, Isaiah 63:16 and 64:8, Jeremiah 3:19, and a few other places. It is also found in prayers of the synagogue. See *Theological Dictionary of the New Testament*, edited by Gerhard Friedrich, (Grand Rapids: Eerdmans. 1967) Vol. 5, p. 978.

9. Article 1, *The Articles of Religion*, BCP p. 867

original speaker intended. To introduce the simile of God as mother, for example, into our liturgical repertoire, not as a substitute for Father, but as a means of reminding ourselves that the attributes of divine fatherhood which we invoke are unrelated to gender or sex, is one way to attempt to manifest a more complete image of God in the liturgy. "As a mother cares for her children . . ." is certainly an image of the divine concern for us as God's children. It does not destroy the metaphor of the God and Father of our Lord Jesus Christ, but it gives us a fuller and more comprehensive picture, one more intimate and personal than "Creator."

In fact, many of the images of God used in the liturgy are "masculine," and have been historically conditioned by the patriarchal nature not only of Jewish society, but of much of Christian society. If we believe that this reflects cultural bias, and is not a part of the gospel, then the deliberate introduction of complementary "feminine" images to our worship is desirable.

This is clearly preferable to the removal of the "masculine" images, many of which are deeply embedded in both Scripture and Tradition. Removing masculine images often depersonalizes worship and theology as does the substitution of gender-free abstractions. What is needed is not the impoverishment but the enrichment of the language of prayer.

The Continuing Theological and Linguistic Exploration

When the contemporary language Rite Two was added to the Cranmerian Rite One in the 1979 Book of Common Prayer, some worshipers mourned the loss of familiar language and the images and turns of phrase with which they had become familiar over the years, and which had formed their devotional and theological thought. To them Donald Parsons, then Bishop of Quincy, addressed his devotional commentary, *The Holy Eucharist: Rite Two*, to "show that the new liturgy also has phrases which speak to our condition, [and] that it is possible to pray the Second Service too and not just suffer under it."[10] Many who considered the authorization of new alternatives imperative in 1973 do not see the force of the same argument today. The liturgy does speak to their condition, and they see no reason to introduce new language. Yet Parsons' message is intended for them also.

One of the advantages of new liturgical texts, especially those which use different images, is that they disrupt our easy familiarity with traditional phrases and challenge us to think afresh about what we really mean by the words we use. They call us not to abandon traditional faith, but to look and see what new and enriching patterns of devotion which our present rite does not afford us are offered by the supplementary texts.

The way we pray really does shape the way we think. The images and metaphors and just plain words we use in our prayer, much more than our reading of

---

10. New York: Seabury Press. 1976, p. 2

Origen or Tillich or Ricoeur or Segundo, tend to shape our faith and our thought. And since all such images are to some degree inadequate, it is wise to have a good collection of them.

The figure of Christ as the Divine Wisdom, the Hagia Sophia after whom Constantine named his great church in Constantinople, has a distinguished pedigree, but has not appeared often in liturgical prayer. A new canticle from Wisdom 10 uses this as its primary metaphor, and the joint work of Wisdom and Spirit in creation find a place in the Second Supplemental Eucharistic Prayer. The imagery from Hosea 11, of God teaching Israel to walk and leading them with "cords of compassion and bands of love," is another vivid biblical image showing a different aspect of God's care for us.

Some aspects of this restoration of neglected metaphors are problematical. "Creator" is not really a synonym for "Father" any more than "creature" is a synonym for "child." God is our creator, and the creator of the entire cosmos, but we are also God's children "by adoption and grace," and that is different and speaks of a different relationship, a relationship in the Christ who called God "Abba."

The meaning of the persons of the Trinity as Father, Son, and, Holy Spirit stands at the core of Christian theological tradition, and the Gloria Patri was painfully fought out in the patristic Church as the liturgical expression of the praise of the Triune God. The frequently-used alternative, naming the Trinity as Creator, Redeemer, and Sanctifier, appears to equate divine activities which are properly ascribed to the joint activity of the three persons, with the persons themselves. The problem, if not its solution, has been well stated by Gail Ramshaw:

> We can of course speak carefully and reverently of a God beyond sexuality, but the result of retaining masculine references for Christ is to admit a linguistic distinction which threatens the Nicean faith . . . Nicea sought to articulate the faith that God assumed humanity so that humanity might be saved. Our task is to find language which is both orthodox — which affirms "Yes we accept the Christian faith" — and kerygmatic — which suggests "This is how we say that faith in our tongue.". . . The most difficult question remains virtually unaddressed: is there a way to speak of the Trinity with more inclusive yet still orthodox terms.[11]

A most difficult problem, hinted at earlier, is the use of masculine pronouns to, refer to God. To the extent that this traditional usage of English grammar causes worshipers to think of God as male or causes women to feel that their creation in God's image is being denied, it is a serious distortion of the meaning of what is being proclaimed. Fortunately, the liturgy normally addresses God directly, and second person pronouns are not gender specific in English, but the psalms,

---

11. Gail Ramshaw-Schmidt, "Naming the Trinity: Orthodoxy and Inclusivity," *Worship* 60 (1986) pp. 491f.

canticles, and biblical readings frequently call God "he." English, unlike many other ancient and modern languages, does not readily distinguish between grammatical gender and the sex of the antecedent. French has no difficulty with the idea that "army" and "beard" are grammatically feminine, nor German with the notion that "girl" is neuter. But English does not really have grammatical gender, and in contemporary usage "he" is increasingly used exclusively to refer to male persons and "she" to female, while "it" implies an inanimate object. Sexual identification is so much a part of the way we experience other persons that we lack the vocabulary to speak of someone in nonsexual but personal terms. To some extent the problem can be avoided by rephrasing sentences, but eliminating the use of pronouns altogether interrupts the flow of the language.

Expanding the Language of Liturgy

In short, these supplemental prayers make a beginning at providing a fuller feast of images which may help us to rehabilitate some that have been worn out with overuse, or distorted through standing alone. Their use can be a real opportunity for spiritual growth. The Holy and Undivided Trinity whom we worship as Father, Son, and Holy Spirit is the same God to whom all of the other metaphors are applied. They do not diminish, but expand our approach to the source of all being, who is revealed to us in the vastness of interstellar space, in the complexity of sub-atomic particles, and in the warmth of human love, yet took flesh in the womb of Mary and became one of us, the divine-human person Jesus, who died for us upon the Cross and was raised again that we might share in the divine life.

2. Introduction

The services contained in *Prayer Book Studies 30 — Supplemental Liturgical Texts* were drafted in response to a resolution of the General Convention of 1985, requiring that the Standing Liturgical Commission "prepare inclusive language liturgies for the regular services of the Church, i.e. Morning and Evening Prayer and the Holy Eucharist . . ." At the next Convention, in 1988, the Commission was directed to "continue to study, develop, and evaluate supplemental inclusive-language liturgical texts . ."

These texts represent the Church's initial response to these resolutions, and to the changing needs of the people of God and the dynamic character of the English language within the prayer of the Church. The need for a more "inclusive" language liturgy, becoming increasingly important for more and more in the Church, was clearly expressed in a survey prepared by the Committee for the Full Participation of Women in the Church, reported to the Convention in 1988. Titled *Reaching Toward Wholeness: The Participation of Women in the Episcopal*

Church, it covered many subjects, including "Image and Language" (the third section). Its findings include:

> The conditions, attitudes and values of every society are reflected in its language and imagery. As the primary mode of communication, language determines what can and cannot be expressed, and shapes the tone of that expression (page 27).

> We find that traditional English usage tends either to render women invisible, by subsuming them as a subcategory of "man" . . . or to trivialize or degrade them through association with qualities which are less valued in the society than those associated with male terms (e.g., seamstress vs. craftsman, soft vs. hardy, weak vs. strong) (page 28).

> The problem is compounded many times over in the case of language about God. Despite the existence in Scripture of a wide variety of terms and images — including feminine images — for God, traditional liturgies and theological discourse throughout the centuries have used masculine terminology almost exclusively in reference to God. Though few would insist that God is male, the discomfort felt by so many at the idea of addressing God as "Mother" as well as "Father" suggests that the constant use of masculine metaphors does lead us unconsciously to identify God with characteristics associated with male human beings (page 28).

The committee's survey of lay and ordained men and women, regarding the use of inclusive language, led to the following suggestion:

> When women function sacramentally and administratively in roles traditionally filled by men, the inadequacies of our traditional male-dominated language become more apparent, especially to women, and the need to stretch the language to be more inclusive becomes more urgently felt (page 31).

The liturgies contained in Prayer Book Studies 30 deliberately seek a more balanced imagery in descriptions of God. Care has been taken to avoid an over-reliance on metaphors and attributes generally perceived as masculine, and to seek out and use images which describe God in feminine and other scripturally-based terms.

Two different approaches were taken in the development of the texts for the Daily Offices and the Eucharistic rite. Since the Daily Office consists primarily of biblical texts, the process of producing texts for the prayer of the Daily Office required either new translations of existing materials, or searching the Scriptures to provide new texts. The work on the eucharistic rites demanded the writing of entirely new prayers, using images uncovered by a similar search of the Scriptures.

The ELLC Texts

A number of the texts in Prayer Book Studies 30 are the work of the ecumenical English Language Liturgical Consultation (ELLC). Formed in 1985, the Consultation consists of representatives of the major English-speaking churches throughout the world, including the Episcopal and other Anglican churches. Its initial task was to review the work of its predecessor, the International Consultation on English Texts (ICET), in the light of "growing indications that these texts are in need of some revision." The ICET texts themselves were set forth in final form in 1975 in a booklet entitled *Prayers We Have in Common*. Most of these texts were subsequently incorporated into the 1979 Prayer Book.

ELLC texts in PBS 30 which are revisions of the ICET texts are: the Benedictus, Magnificat, Te Deum, Gloria in excelsis, Apostles' Creed, Nicene Creed, Suffrages C at Morning Prayer, and the Sursum corda.

The Daily Office

The majority of the texts traditionally associated with the Office find their source in the Bible. The Psalms and most of the Canticles originate there; opening sentences, opening versicles, invitatory antiphons, and suffrages are drawn from Scripture. The Collects of the Offices echo biblical texts.

The first task, then, in adapting the forms of the Office was to establish the accuracy of the translations of the Hebrew or Greek original. In some instances, male-oriented language for God was used in translations where it does not appear in the original text, such as in Canticles 14 and 20. Terms such as "fathers" were changed to "forebears" in some canticles, to be inclusive of both men and women.

A second task involved working with biblical translations. Texts were amended so that they would provide a more inclusive liturgical wording while remaining faithful to the content of the passage. In some cases, masculine terms and pronouns referring to God have been changed; however, not all masculine references to God have been omitted. The terms "Father" and "Lord" are expressions of biblical faith and have, for the most part, been retained, but an attempt has been made to provide a broader and more balanced use of language referring to God through additional biblical metaphors. Some prayers are recast in direct address (using the second person pronoun). See the ELLC version of the Magnificat and the Benedictus in PBS 30. Following the precedent of the Prayer Book Psalter (see BCP, page 583), the word "Lord," when used as a substitute for YHWH in opening sentences and Old Testament canticles, is printed in large and small capital letters.

All references to the human community have been adapted to be inclusive of both men and women. Masculine pronouns and some masculine terms are therefore no longer used in phrases of general human reference.

The third task involved finding new texts to expand the range of metaphors which are used to speak of God. Two Canticles from the Wisdom literature introduce feminine imagery for God. A new blessing has been included in the Order of Worship for the Evening, as well as opening sentences, invitatory antiphons, and a new set of suffrages for Morning Prayer.

New and revised texts are intended to be alternatives or additions to the existing BCP rites of the Daily Office. This is reflected in the numbering of the Canticles. Canticles which are revisions of existing BCP canticles use the BCP number followed by an "A." The two new Canticles are identified as Canticle 22 and Canticle 23, following in numerical order after the last BCP Canticle.

Morning Prayer

New Opening Sentences

Advent (Baruch 5:5) a sentence with an emphasis on the theme of expectation and the eschatological nature of the season, without masculine imagery.

Christmas (John 1:14) a new sentence which incorporates the metaphor of the Word.

Holy Week (Philippians 2:8) a new sentence centered on the sacrifice of the Cross.

Occasions of Thanksgiving (Psalm 75:1) an acclamation of praise without gender-related language.

At Any Time (John 4:24) a new sentence which identifies God as Spirit.

Confession of Sin

Identical with BCP, except for the use of the term "Savior" in line 9.

Absolution

The phrase "power of the Holy Spirit" is here balanced with a specific reference to "the grace of Jesus Christ."

Alternative Opening Versicle

A new option, based on Psalm 71:8.

Alternative to the Gloria Patri

Honor and glory to the holy and undivided Trinity,*
    God who creates, redeems, and inspires:

One in Three and Three in One,*
    for ever and ever. Amen.

This alternative provides an expression of praise to the Triune God. As noted in the introduction, Trinitarian language is a very perplexing issue. We are challenged with being faithful to the creedal tradition of the Church, while, at the same time, naming the God who is "One in Three and Three in One" in non-gender specific terms.

The use of "honor and glory" deliberately distinguishes the alternative from the Gloria Patri. "Honor and glory" comes from the Mozarabic form, "Gloria et honor Patri, et Filio, et Spiritui Sancto." The order of the words, "honor and glory," is familiar to us from the endings of Prayer Book Rite Two Eucharistic Prayers A and B. The alternative to the Gloria Patri is provided at the beginning of Morning and Evening Prayer, and at the end of the Psalmody. It may, when desired, be used at the end of Canticles for which a Gloria Patri is printed in the BCP.

Invitatory Antiphons

The Latin original of the second half of these antiphons, "Venite adoremus," contains no masculine pronoun. The translation provided is taken from the Canadian Book of Alternative Services (BAS), and retains the number of syllables required for Anglican chant. The Lutheran Book of Worship also retains the "O."

Advent "God" is substituted for "King."

Epiphany "Lord" is changed to "Christ" to match the Latin original.

Lent "The Lord" is changed to "our God" as consistent with the psalm passage.

An alternative antiphon "Today . . ." derives from the text of Psalm 95. It is an ancient antiphon for Lent.

Trinity Sunday A new antiphon which is not gender-related.

Other Sundays A new antiphon which clearly identifies Sunday as the day of resurrection.

Other Sundays and Weekdays Two new antiphons which identify God as the Rock of our salvation and as the Holy One.

The Morning Psalm

Psalm 63:1-8 is provided as an alternative to the present texts. This is a traditional morning psalm and is used as an alternative in the Canadian BAS. It does not refer to God in masculine terms.

Canticles

Canticle 9A In the second line of the first verse, the words "in him" do not occur in the Hebrew original.

Canticle 12A The refrain has been translated with verbs which do not require an object. "In the high vault of heaven, glorify the Lord" restores the text of the original Latin doxology.

Canticle 14A In line 10, the Greek speaks of "Lord" and "Most High." The Prayer Book text preferred "Lord;" here "Most High" is used. In line 17, "O Lord" does not appear in the Greek.

Canticle 15A The text of the Magnificat is an ELLC translation recommended to the churches. It addresses God in the second, rather than the third person. As precedent for such a change, see the Sanctus. The text in Isaiah 6 reads "full of his glory." For liturgical use, the "his" has been changed to "your."

Canticle 16A An ELLC translation which also addresses God in the second person.

Canticle 18A The Prayer Book translation of this Canticle paraphrases the original text; this translation is also paraphrastic and has the advantage of being more inclusive: "Royal power," "O God Most High," "royal priesthood," and "the One."

Canticle 20A This ELLC text is identical with the BCP (ICET) text, except for the substitution of "God's" for "his" in the second line.

Canticle 21A An ELLC translation which is closer to the familiar Rite One version than the ICET version.

Two new Canticles provide references to God using feminine metaphors:

Canticle 22 A Song of Wisdom (Wisdom 10:15-19, 20b-21) A translation from the original Greek of a text which is also found in the Canadian BAS. God's salvation is found through Wisdom, who leads her people through the Red Sea and makes for herself a holy people.

Canticle 23 A Song of Pilgrimage (Ecclesiasticus 51:13-22) A canticle which seeks Wisdom and recognizes in her gift the offering of praise and glory, and the living of one's life in her way. This song is found in the Mozarabic Psalter and has been newly translated from the Latin.

The Apostles' Creed

The ELLC text.

Alternative to the Salutation

Drawn from Psalm 61:1. The use of a supplicatory verse at this point, in place of the salutation, was common in medieval forms of the Office. See BCP Noonday and Compline.

Suffrages B

A new set of suffrages which avoids gender-specific imagery for God. Sources are Psalms 79:9, 74:2, 29:11b, 96:3, 74:20a, 74:18b, 36:10, 90:14.

Suffrages C (BCP "B")
An ELLC translation. The last line has been conformed more closely to the Latin original.

Collects

Some Collects have been changed to provide greater balance in the use of terms describing God. In particular, some of them conclude with "Jesus Christ our Savior" so that not all will end "through Jesus Christ our Lord.". The phrase "through Jesus Christ our Savior" has historical precedent. The 1549 BCP uses a variety of short endings for Collects, and it seems desirable to continue that tradition.

Collects for Friday and for Saturday "Lord" has been changed to "Savior," which more adequately reflects the saving event of the Cross.

Collect for Guidance "O God our Creator and Sustainer" reflects the God in whom "we live and move and have our being." See Acts 17:22-28.

Prayer of St. Chrysostom

A new rendering of the Greek text. English versions of this prayer have always been problematical, and it is suspected by some scholars that Archbishop Cranmer may have had a defective text before him. The Greek is based on Matthew 18:19, which specifically speaks of *agreeing*, and not just *gathering*, as the basis for our requests being answered. The Greek, moreover, is addressed to Christ, as is Cranmer's translation.

Concluding Sentences

Third alternative "Glory to God" provides a more vigorous statement.

An Order of Worship for the Evening

Opening Acclamations

New acclamations for Lent and Easter Season are provided which do not use the term "Lord."

Short Lessons

Matthew 5:14-16 "Among other people" takes the place of "among your fellow men," and accurately reflects the sense of the Greek.

2 Corinthians 4:5-6 The Revised Standard Version of the passage is used in place of the New English Bible, since it is more inclusive and retains the image of the heart, which is also used in the first prayer that follows.

Psalm 139:10-11 "O God" is substituted for "O Lord." Neither phrase is in the Hebrew, but is a Prayer Book addition made for clarity.

Prayers for Light

The changes made are consistent with the changes made in the Collects of Morning Prayer.

Psalms 134 and 141

See the comments below under Evening Prayer.

Concluding Prayers

In the first prayer, "O Lord our God" takes the place of "O Lord, the God of our fathers."

In the second prayer, the opening petition has been conformed to the Prayer Book translation of Psalm 141, which this adaptation has added to the service.

Blessing

An alternative has been added, taken from the Book of Worship of the United Church of Canada.

Evening Prayer

For comments about most of the contents of this service, see above under "The Daily Office" and "Morning Prayer."

Alternatives to Phos hilaron

Psalm 134 is a traditional evening psalm used as an invitatory in the *Alternative Service Book* of the Church of England and in the Canadian BAS. While it uses the word "Lord" it contains no masculine overtones.

Prayers for Mission

In the first prayer, "Maker" is substituted for "Father" as congruent with the petitions that follow. "Men and women" is changed to "people" to be inclusive of children as well as adults.

The Holy Eucharist

The eucharistic rite contained in Prayer Book Studies 30 is newly composed. The rite follows the same order as the Rite Two eucharist in the BCP, and is related to the classical content of the ancient Christian liturgical rites as authorized in the 1979 BCP. Variable prayers are provided for the collect, prayers of the people, eucharistic prayers, and postcommunion prayer.

Opening Acclamation

According to the practice established by the 1979 BCP, the service opens with one of three acclamations:

> "Blessed be the one, holy, and living God" acclaims the Trinity as Unity through its structure of three adjectives describing the one God. God is "one," as in the traditional Judeo-Christian vision of God the Father; "holy," suggesting the sanctification of the Incarnate One; and "living," recalling both the risen Christ and the eternal and living presence of the Holy Spirit. The response, "Glory to God for ever and ever," echoes the response from Rite Two, Prayer C, and its doxological antecedents.

Easter Season: The simple phrases of the Easter acclamation incorporate the Alleluias traditional to the season. The versicle is an elegantly simple proclamation, "Blessed be our God," recalling the song of Zechariah (Luke 1:68ff: "Blessed be the Lord, the God of Israel; for he has come to his people and set them free . . ."). The response, "Christ is risen," echoes the traditional Eastern Orthodox acclamation.

Lent: "Blessed be the God of our salvation" applies the familiar Old Testament characterization of God as "God of our salvation" (Psalm 68:19,20 among others, where "salvation" translates *yeshuah*, or "Jesus") to penitential seasons. The response, "Who bears our burdens and forgives our sins," carries manifold allusions: to the "Suffering Servant" of Isaiah 53, who has "borne our griefs and carried our sorrows;" to Jesus bearing the cross, whose "yoke is easy" and whose "burden is light" (Matthew 11:30); and to the continuing Judeo-Christian vision of God as the one who forgives sins (see, notably, Jeremiah 31:34; Matthew 6:12; Mark 2:7).

Song of Praise

The Song of Praise included here, the Supplemental Texts' translation of Canticle 18, the Song of the Lamb (from the Revelation), is particularly suitable for use in worship in which inclusion of all peoples is being emphasized. The other alternative provided, the Trisagion, seems strikingly modern in its gender-free language about God, yet it has been in continuous use in the liturgical tradition since at least the fifth century. Like the opening acclamation, its threefold structure suggests the Trinity in unity. The petition "have mercy upon us" makes it especially suitable for penitential occasions.

The Salutation

Historic liturgies show considerable variety in the wording of the salutation. A simple alternative, "God be with you," is suggested here.

The Collect of the Day

The Collect of the Day or one of three alternative Collects is offered.

The opening phrase of the first Collect, "O God, who wonderfully created and yet more wonderfully restored the dignity of human nature," is taken from the Collect after the first reading at the Easter Vigil (BCP page 288) and the Collect for the Second Sunday after Christmas (BCP page 214). The middle part is written to acknowledge Jesus as God in the fullness of humanity; the title in the conclusion, "Anointed One," reflects Acts 10:38 and has baptismal overtones.

The second Collect relates the Paschal sacraments of Baptism and Eucharist to the Christian mission in the world. Those who have been "reborn" and "anointed" in Baptism are continually "nourished" in communion to show forth the love of God in the world through the Spirit of the Risen Christ.

The third Collect addresses God as Creator, a significant image of God in the Hebrew Scriptures. Further, God is addressed as "fountain of light and love and life," recalling Jeremiah's oracle describing God as "the fountain of living water" (Jeremiah 17:13), an image echoed in the vision of the New Jerusalem in Revelation (21:6 — "To the thirsty I will give from the fountain of the water of life without payment"), recalling, in turn, Isaiah's "Ho, every one who thirsts, come to the waters" (55:1). The "fountain of life" and image of "light" also has roots in the ancient prayer of St. Basil (Eucharistic Prayer D, BCP page 372f).

The petition "Be near to us, and embrace us; and teach us to walk in your truth and your ways," draws on a variety of scriptural sources. The image of God as one who embraces and teaches us is shaped principally by Hosea's oracle of God as the one "who taught Ephraim to walk . . . (who) took them up in my arms" (Hosea 11:3); by Isaiah's image of God as the shepherd who will tenderly "gather the lambs in his arms . . . carry them in his bosom" (Isaiah 40:11); and by Jesus' lament over Jerusalem, "how often I would have gathered you as a hen gathers her brood under her wings" (Matthew 23:37), a maternal image of embracing and holding close. In the Prayer Book tradition, this image of embrace recalls Bishop Brent's prayer, the third for mission in the morning office: ". . you stretched out your arms of love on the hard wood of the cross that everyone might come within the reach of your saving embrace." The petition to "teach us to walk in your truth and your ways" echoes Psalm 86:11, "teach me your way, O Lord, and I will walk in your truth," as well as the familiar saying of Jesus, "I am the way, the truth, and the life" (John 14:6).

The Nicene Creed

An ELLC translation. This version follows the Greek original precisely in translating line 15 as "was incarnate of the Holy Spirit and the Virgin Mary," thus emphasizing that Mary was an active, rather than a passive, participant in the Incarnation

(Luke 1:38). Some early Latin manuscripts agree with this and read "et Maria Virgine." The version which prevailed, however, changed the "et" to "ex."

This version also follows the Greek and Latin (and the English of Rite One) in using "who" rather than "he" in the section, about the Holy Spirit.

The Prayers of the People

Prayer is offered with intercession for the Church and for the world. As in the Rite Two Eucharist of the BCP, prayers may be written for the occasion using the categories listed (BCP pages 359 and 383); offered using one of the forms found in Prayer Book Studies 30 (Prayers of the People First and Second Supplements, pages 54-57); or Forms I through VI in the BCP (pages 383-393).

Confession of Sin and Absolution

This prayer of confession emphasizes the fact that sin prevents our living fully in the image of God with which we have been blessed, and which is the promise given and received at Baptism. The Absolution is the form used in Morning and Evening Prayer.

The Peace

Historically, the formula used to introduce the exchange of the peace has varied widely. The text used here underscores the fact that it is the peace of the Risen Christ that is referred to (John 20:19, 26).

The Great Thanksgiving

Two eucharistic prayers are provided in the rite. The First Supplemental Prayer emphasizes the doctrine of our creation in the image of God — understanding that the source of inclusiveness in the Christian tradition is to be found in the reality that all people are created in the image of God. The Second Supplemental Prayer uses the metaphor of God giving birth to, and nurturing, the whole creation.

Both eucharistic prayers have a common Sursum corda and Sanctus. The Sursum corda is the proposed ELLC version and is also used in the Canadian BAS. The Sanctus is a slightly revised version of the traditional hymn. The principal change is in the Benedictus: "Blessed is the one who comes in the name of our God."

First Supplemental Eucharistic Prayer

The fixed preface of the First Supplemental Eucharistic Prayer gives thanks that we are made in God's image, are remembered by God, are redeemed in Christ, and replenished by the Spirit. After the Sanctus, the prayer continues in thanksgiving for the generous "self-giving" love of God.

We who are made in the image of God acknowledge the responsibility of being made stewards of God's creation (Genesis 1:26-28) and the task of revealing the infinite love which has been given to us.

The history of salvation is recalled, beginning with the covenant relationship between God and humanity "through Abraham and Sarah" (Genesis 17:1, 15-19), extending through the Exodus, "You delivered us from slavery, prepared us in the wilderness" (Exodus), and proclaimed through the prophets (see also Luke 1:68-79). The past is brought forward to include all of us; this is our salvation history and our present story.

"But we failed to honor your image in one another and in ourselves . . . in the world around us" speaks of the awareness that the first step in the dynamics of exclusion is to see others as "not like us," which in the Christian tradition would mean "not made in the image of God" (Luke 18:10-14). The failure to honor creation gives rise to those sinful actions in which we "violate creation," "abuse one another," and "reject" God's love. "Yet you did not abandon us to sin and death, but sent Jesus Christ to be our Savior" speaks of the redemptive love of God for all of creation (John 3:16,17; 1 Timothy 1:15; John 2:1,2).

The fullness of the incarnation is unfolded in the active verbs concerning Jesus: "Walking among us," "touched us," "showed us," and "giving himself freely" for our salvation.

One marked change in the words of institution is the shift from the blood "shed for you and for many" to the blood "poured out for you and for all." "Poured out" is an equally good translation of the Greek, chosen as a better rendering of the double levels of significance: blood is "poured out" from a wound, and wine is also "poured out."

The change from "many" to "all" has been urged by many biblical scholars for some time, as a more faithful translation of the meaning of the Greek.[*] This change makes it clear that forgiveness of sins is available to *all* through Christ's sacrifice. This change is also to be found in the Second Supplemental Eucharistic Prayer.

"Friends," rather than disciples, allows for the weighty arguments that the term "disciples" is often mistaken to refer only to the Twelve and that there may have been women at the Last Supper.

The three-fold memorial acclamation presents a progression in the nature and work of Christ. The human person Jesus, clearly a man, is remembered for "*his*" death on the cross. The resurrection "we proclaim" is not the resurrection of

---

[*] [Editor's Note: Regrettably, no citations have been provided here. The standard meaning for the Greek word "*polus*" in this text is "many"; "*pas*" would be the typical choice for "all."]

the Christ alone, but of all for whom Christ's resurrection has destroyed death: thus "*the* resurrection." And finally, we await "the return of Christ" in glory, understanding that the return of Christ will not be primarily the appearance of a male person but a manifestation of the fullness of redeemed humanity. This acclamation is also found in the Second Supplemental Eucharistic Prayer.

We pray that God will "remember" and "welcome" us, which recalls God's transcendence and the incorporation of all people, past, present, and yet to come, into the holy heritage begun at our creation and to be fulfilled in the *eschaton*. It also completes the inclusive *anamnetic* imagery: We remember because God has remembered through all time and will remember us in eternity (Luke 1:54,55).

Second Supplemental Eucharistic Prayer

The preface begins with an echo of the opening acclamation, "O holy and living God," who is addressed as Creator. Three proper prefaces are provided, each one emphasizing a different person of the Trinity.

The first proper preface offers praise to the First Person of the Trinity as universal Creator and the one who engenders the new creation (2 Corinthians 5:17).

The second echoes Rite Two, Prayer D, in quoting John 3:16: "Father, you loved the world so much . . . you sent your only Son," emphasizing the incarnate life of Christ in Jesus.

The third preface plays on the linguistic connection between "breath" and "spirit," recalling the Creation story (Genesis 2:7) and the risen Christ in the upper room breathing on the disciples that they might receive the Holy Spirit (John 20: 19-23). "Guardian and guide" are attributes of the "Counselor" of Isaiah 9:6 and John 14:16-26. "Fullness of life in Christ" is rooted in Colossians 2:9-10, John 1:16, and Ephesians 4:13.

The prayer continues with a list of the hosts of heaven who are the choir of the "chorus of praise." It is lengthened from the more familiar brief catalogue ("angels and archangels") to the more expansive "angels and archangels, prophets and martyrs, and all the holy men and women loved by you who have entered into joy." This expansion is in the spirit of the early Liturgies of St. James and St. Basil, which include long lists of the members of the heavenly host, surely to excite worshipers' awe about the vastness of the chorus with whom "we join."

"O God, from before time . . . your children." This capsule account of the creation follows the order set out in Genesis 1, and gives special emphasis to the image of God as both male and female (Genesis 1:26-27). The role of the human race in creation is depicted after the pattern of the loving and caring God, the benevolent ruler rather than powerful despot. Wisdom, whose role in the divine order is detailed in the great hymns of Ecclesiasticus (Sirach) 24:1-29 and Wisdom of Solomon 6:12—11:1, is the feminine *Sophia* and is here identified with the *Logos* or Divine Word (as in John 1:1ff). In this understanding of creation, the Spirit moving over the waters was empowered through Wisdom.

In the paragraph, "You graced us . . . the fullness of your love," "freedom of heart and mind" elaborates "the glorious liberty of the children of God" (Romans 8:21). Perhaps the most vivid image recalled by "You took us by the hand" is Michaelangelo's Sistine Chapel ceiling rendering of the hands of God and Adam reaching toward each other at creation. From Hosea 11:3-4 comes the image of God teaching us to walk, leading us with "cords of compassion and bands of love." "As a mother cares for her children" draws upon Isaiah's oracle of God as a nursing mother (Isaiah 49:15-16) as well as the image of Christ as the mother hen with her brood (Matthew 23:37). The "fullness of your love" again suggests the New Testament proclamation of *pleroma*, "fullness," alluded to in the third proper preface. "Then you acted anew . . . the holy child of God." To "see and know" implies the fullest possible experience; the phrase is familiar from the Collect for ordinations in BCP 1979 ("Let the whole world see and know . . ."). The full union of Mary and the Spirit in the Incarnation is underscored here, as in the restored text of the Nicene Creed's assertion that "he became incarnate by the Holy Spirit and the Virgin Mary."

A series of sentences, "seasonal embolisms," are provided for insertion into the Christological section of the Eucharistic Prayer to correlate the prayer more specifically with the aspects of the life and work of Jesus being remembered at the particular period in the Church year.

The *Advent* sentence concentrates on waiting "in pain and hope" (Romans 8:18-24; Hebrews 10:13), and interprets the Incarnation as the fulfillment of God's ancient promise in the covenant (cf. the promise to Abraham and Sarah, Genesis 18, Romans 9, Ephesians 3:6; and Jeremiah's "new covenant," Jeremiah 31:31-34).

The *Christmas* sentence echoes "lowly" from the Magnificat, "wisdom and stature" from Luke 2:52, and the vivid phrase "the apple of your eye" — familiar from Compline — from Psalm 17:8.

The *Epiphany* sentence uses the traditional image of light.

The *Baptism* sentence is included here for use on the Sunday of the Baptism of Our Lord. The mention of Jesus' baptism by "his cousin John" points up the family relationship, in keeping with the motif of relationship and family that runs through this eucharistic prayer.

The sentence for *Lent* emphasizes the humanity of Jesus as one who participated fully in our human life, "who was tempted as we are, yet without sin" (Hebrews 4:15).

The rush of active verbs ("came, suffered, died, rising, opened the way") in the *Easter* sentence emphasizes the dynamic movement of this crowning season of the year, encapsulating the essence of the work of Christ. The connection is drawn with the New Creation (2 Corinthians 5:17) as the realm opened by the reconciliation made by Christ in the Easter event.

The theme of fullness, *pleroma*, recurs in the *Ascension* sentence, as the eschatological fullness effected by the Christ in majesty, in which we are promised eventual participation in the place prepared for us (John. 14:2; Matthew 25:34).

Both traditional images of the Holy Spirit — breath (John 20:2.2) and fire (Acts 2) — are included in the *Pentecost* sentence, along with the reminder that the gift of the Holy Spirit is for a purpose: "to live the gospel life."

The Eucharistic Prayer continues (after the seasonal embolism) with the first explicit use of Jesus' image of himself as the mother hen (Matthew 23:37, Luke 13:34). This completes the Christological section of the prayer and leads into the institution narrative.

The institution narrative begins with an emphasis on Christ's own self-offering, following the sacrificial theology of Hebrews 10 (echoed in Cranmer's "his one oblation of himself, once offered . . ."). The language of "at table with his friends" again emphasizes familiarity and relationship. As in the First Supplemental Eucharistic Prayer, there has been a shift from the blood "shed for you and for many" to the blood "poured out for you and for all."

The memorial acclamation is identical with that found in the First Supplemental Eucharistic Prayer.

The oblation formula seeks to use concrete and specific language about what our offering includes: bread and wine, our money, and our time. The specific mention of "money" is optional, since not all eucharistic celebrations include a money offering.

A number of themes and images reappear in the invocation of the Holy Spirit. "Pour out your love and blessing" echoes the blood "poured out" in the words over the cup. The Spirit/ Breath identification and the Spirit in creation also are reprises of earlier images. The use of "brood" as the action of the Spirit in creation is a rendering of the "movement" of the Spirit in Genesis 1:2 and of the same Spirit in Romans 8, who indwells in us; and echoes the "brood" that the hen would gather under her wings in Jesus' image of himself. The creation theme is again sounded in "the world you have made." The image of "the heart of the world" is familiar from English Renaissance poetry; to be drawn to God's "heart at the heart of the world" alludes to the intimacy of pregnancy, when infants are carried just below their mothers' heart, and evokes other senses of embracing and security.

Fraction Anthem

The first fraction anthem, "We are the body of Christ," comments on the action of breaking the bread, so that the relationship between the assembled people of God (the Body of Christ) and the consecrated Bread as the Body of Christ is revealed. This anthem is rooted in the writings of St. Augustine: "The Lord willed to impart his Body, and his blood which he shed for the remission of sins. If you have received well, you are what you have received" (Sermon 22.7). "Your mystery is laid on the table of the Lord; your mystery you receive. To what you are, you answer 'Amen,' and in answering you assent. For you hear the words 'The

Body of Christ' and you answer 'Amen.' Be a member of the Body of Christ that the Amen may be true" (Sermon 272).

The second anthem articulates and weaves together two central themes of baptismal life. The first, that we are members of the Body of Christ. When we break the bread "Is it not a participation in the body of Christ? Because there is one bread, we who are many are one body, for we all partake of the one bread" (1 Corinthians 10:16,17). The second is the Gospel imperative of the Last Supper account in John, "Love one another" (John 13:34).

Postcommunion prayer

In Baptism we have been made new, reborn in the fullness of creation, restored to the image of God. In the Eucharist, our, baptismal union with God in Christ is renewed in and through the "Sacrament of Christ's Body and Blood." We pray that we may be empowered to live the life of Christ in the world.

The second prayer begins with a threefold address to God, similar to the opening acclamation. The structure of the prayer is (1) drawing in, (2) feeding, (3) sending forth, (4) proclaiming, set out in simple language with themes repeated from the Second Supplemental Eucharistic Prayer.

Prayers of the People – First Supplemental Form

The content of the prayers offered in the First Supplemental intercession is rooted in the biblical understanding of creation found in the First Supplemental Eucharistic Prayer.

Therefore it is suggested for use with that prayer, but is not limited to it. The first petition prays for the people of God, who are empowered by the Holy Spirit to show forth the life of Christ in the world (Matthew 28:19-20; Mark 16:15; Acts 1:8). The words of the Baptismal Covenant: "Will you proclaim by word and example the Good News of God in Christ?" (BCP page 305) are recalled in the petition.

Prayer for the whole creation is offered with the awareness that we have been entrusted with the stewardship of creation (Genesis 1:26-31). We exercise a stewardship which is grounded in the love of God who has created all things and who has said "it was good" (Genesis 1:1ff).

The Christian responsibilities of stewardship extend throughout our lives: in our work, our play, and in the authority we exercise in the decision-making processes of the market place and the governing of our communities and our nation. We acknowledge our commitment to be servants of God and of one another (Matthew 23:11; Mark 9:35; John 12:26).

We pray for the renewal of our hearts to the awareness of God's image found in the faces of all people (Genesis 1:26-28; Matthew 22:39; 25:34-46; Galatians 5:14; Ephesians 3:14-19). In Baptism we promise to "seek and serve Christ" through loving our neighbor (BCP page 305) and so we pray to uphold all relationships, the easy and the difficult (Matthew 5:43-48).

In Baptism we entered into our heritage as the "holy people" (1 Peter 2:9,10) of God and are empowered by the life-giving Spirit (John 20:22; Ezekiel 37:5,9,10) to reveal the love of God in this world. We seek freedom from "lack of vision" (Matthew 23:13-36), "inertia of will and spirit" (Romans 12:2), "isolation and oppression" (Matthew 11:28-30; Mark 5:25-34).

Thanksgiving is offered for the "gift of life," with prayer that God will shield, comfort, strengthen, and bless us throughout our lives, in our birthing and dying, in our joys and our sorrows.

Prayers of the People – Second Supplemental Form

The structure of this prayer is a modified litany, with a gathering line answered by a congregational response, repeated with changes throughout the prayer. The thematic emphasis in the petitions is on relationship and family, and the prayer is suggested for use with the Second Supplemental Eucharistic Prayer.

"We pray for our nation . . ." This petition incorporates language from the American cultural heritage: "a more perfect union" from the United States Constitution. The emphasis here is on the inclusion of all people in God's grace and perfect union, as a fulfillment of the most gracious version of the American ideal.

"We pray for all peoples, tribes, and nations . . ." The mention of "tribes" strikes a significant note of inclusion for many people for whom tribal identification is an important element of "glorious liberty," both in other parts of the world and in the United States. "Glorious liberty" is the "birthright" of the children of God (Romans 8:21).

"We pray for this community . . ." seeks to include specific concerns of children and young people — play and school as well as those of the adult community. "We pray for everyone whose body aches . . ." again seeks to use concrete and specific language, rather than generalities or categorizations ("the sick," "the poor"). "Instruments of your peace" recalls the prayer attributed to St. Francis (BCP page 833).

"We pray for all those who have died . . ." The request to "draw them to your bosom in love" incorporates images from the Second Supplemental Eucharistic Prayer ("Draw us to your heart at the heart of the world") and from the vision of the afterlife as "Abraham's bosom" (Luke z6:22.), an especially rich image in Afro-American religious traditions.

The closing Collect also sounds themes familiar from the Second Supplemental Eucharistic Prayer: creation, birth, life as daughters and sons in the family of God. "Draw us together" is reminiscent of the image from Hosea of being led with "cords of compassion and bands of love" (Hosea 11:4).

3. Guidelines for Parish Use

The use of these texts was authorized by the General Convention in a resolution which indicated that such use be "limited by the direction of ecclesiastical authority." Each diocesan bishop will establish further guidelines than those which follow here; it is imperative that parishes participating in this experimental process do so in consultation with their bishop's office.

Purpose of the Rites

General Convention authorized the use of supplemental texts as one initial step in a careful process toward the supplementation and enrichment of the Book of Common Prayer 1979. The use of the texts during this period is, first of all, meant to be a preliminary step in a process of producing rites which take into account the concerns raised in the "Background" chapter of this Commentary. Participating parishes will contribute to the refining and perfecting of these texts, so that the rites presented to the Convention in 1991 will reflect the response of the Church. A second purpose is the provision of interim texts which make services available to the Church which may be faithfully prayed by those for whom these concerns are immediate and palpable, until such time as the Church agrees on rites which will serve as a supplement to those now contained in the Prayer Book. It is important to note that these texts do not now nor will they in the future replace the present liturgies of the Church. Rather, they are being considered as a way to enrich the liturgy by the addition of texts which, when used regularly, along with existing Prayer Book texts, will restore a more balanced range of imagery for God and will be unambiguously inclusive about the scope of the Church's people and mission.

The Importance of Education

Change in the Church's prayer is not a simple matter. Familiarity is an important aspect of regular liturgical worship, and change therefore comes only with time and use. These texts follow the familiar structure of Morning Prayer, Evening Prayer, and the Holy Eucharist, but introduce into these services biblical images and language that have not been available to the Church's corporate worship until this time. A growing number of worshipers, concerned about offering a balanced and complete language for God and humanity, will find these texts responding to a deepening sense of God's fullness. But for others, this is not an automatic nor an easy process, and those who are involved should expect and welcome a range of responses. This is an exploration into places of prayer that the Church has just begun, and in the beginning the steps may seem to be occasionally unsteady or even, to some, unwelcome. If used not only as prayer, but in and with prayer, it is hoped that these texts will lead to a fuller and deeper knowledge and love of God and of the human race, which is the purpose of all prayer, old and new.

Principles for Use

Becoming familiar with new forms of worship requires time and experience. Most new forms will inevitably seem awkward at first, until with use they become more natural and known. Using only these Supplemental Texts for a long enough period that a congregation becomes familiar with them — for instance, at all Sunday services for a month or two — is therefore recommended as a way to begin. After therites have undergone the initial period of concentrated use, clergy and congregation can better determine how to best incorporate them into their on-going worship life. Many parishes now pray more than one of the Prayer Book Eucharistic Prayers (Prayers A, B, C, or D of Rite Two) seasonally or in some other sequence. The next step with the Supplemental Texts would be to build them into a regular rotation of prayer, since it is the use of the range of prayers available which will serve to make the prayer of the Church more inclusive. No one service can bear that weight alone.

In addition to their use with other Prayer Book services, there may well be special occasions of regular or occasional worship particularly appropriate for their use. Regular weekday worship services, for example, can be excellent opportunities to consider for their regular use, though it is important that they also be used for Sunday worship and not be limited to weekday services.

Evaluation

The chief purpose of the experimental use of the Supplemental Texts is to involve parishes in an extensive process of consultation and response as they are perfected by the Liturgical Commission to present to the Convention in 1991. The period of evaluation will run from late Fall of 1989 into May of 1990 (exact dates to be determined in each diocese). Details about the evaluation process are available from diocesan offices.

Planning and Preparation

The canons of the Church place decisions about parish worship in the hands of the rector. Clergy have found it important, however, to consult with their congregations in planning worship, and many parishes now have worship committees of some sort. These texts will be more effective if parishes plan for their use carefully, which will involve consultation with vestries, worship committees, and education committees. It will also be important to involve parish musicians and music committees in order to integrate music for the new texts into worship effectively (and to be attentive to the choice of hymns, that those used with these services may serve to enhance the worship experience with a wide range of images for God.

Education, consultation, and preparation, using these and other materials, then, may add greatly to the experience of worship with these prayers. Knowledge of their context and how they were created will help them "come alive" for those participating in this crucial experimental stage of development, and will be essential for informed responses by congregations. The Standing Liturgical Commission urges careful and thorough use of all available educational material so that the texts themselves may more fully proclaim the saving acts of God — that the Church's mission will "come alive" in new ways for more and more of God's people.

4. Study Guide

Joseph P. Russell

In this chapter we offer a study guide designed to help introduce the Supplemental Liturgical Texts to congregations or for personal study. A time of preparation is essential if the Supplemental Liturgical Texts are to be used constructively. A study of the texts need not be limited to persons who will be using them in the worship of their congregation. The issue of "inclusive language" in the Church today is an important one, and the study outlined in this guide provides a way of exploring the issue. Moreover, experience shows that a study of the Supplemental Texts leads to a deeper understanding of the Book of Common Prayer and the Episcopal Church's liturgical tradition. Let the introduction of the texts be an opportunity for liturgical study within the diocese and the congregation.

This study guide is designed for a three-session course. The first session provides an overview of the issues that lie behind the Supplemental Liturgical Texts. The second session explores the eucharistic rites of the 1979 Book of Common Prayer so that we may approach the Supplemental Liturgical Texts with a deeper understanding of their significance and have additional tools with which to evaluate the new material. The final session offers a way of introducing the texts found in Prayer Book Studies 30. You may want to change the order of the sessions by exploring the texts first, then studying the rationale that lies behind them, and ending with a study of the Prayer Book eucharistic rites.

A three-session evening course provides the best opportunity to explore the subject in some depth, but Sunday morning is the time when most of the congregation can be present. Offer evening sessions for the worship committee of the congregation and invite other interested persons to participate. Adapt the design for shorter sessions in a Sunday morning series. Diocesan Liturgical

Commissions could offer the sessions in a Saturday workshop setting for congregational teams. This would provide a way of introducing the texts to the diocese and would train persons in the congregation for their work. There may be a problem scheduling Sunday morning adult education in congregations which do not have a regular adult education program. Curiosity about the texts may be the drawing card to get persons involved, and the promise of further dialogue and study might provide enough incentive to maintain an on-going group. Offering breakfast before or after the forum can also be an encouragement to participate.

Children as well as adults need to be prepared for the experience of praying with the texts. Suggestions for children's involvement are included in this study guide. You may want to adapt suggestions made there for use with adults. An option is to offer the course as an intergenerational program using the design for children.

Each session includes lecture material along with a process to help persons explore what they have heard or read. People do not learn simply from what they hear but from reflecting on their own experience, and by talking about their understanding with others. Thus, the work that the group does together is the key to an effective education series. Some of the lecture material offered as a part of each section is taken from other sections of this Commentary. Leaders may have other source material that also seems relevant and helpful. You need to read the entire Commentary as basic background for leading sessions with adults or children. Ideally, you will adapt the content material so that it becomes suited to your own situation, or you may prefer to prepare your own material using the proposed talks simply as an outline. An option is to offer the content as a handout, letting each person read it before or during a session. The bibliography included in the study guide offers a variety of resources to supplement the material found here.

This study guide, of course, is only the beginning of the education process in the diocese and congregation. The learning continues as the texts are prayed. The learning is reinforced as the congregation is drawn together from time to time to reflect on the experience. Guidelines for such reflection times are offered as a part of this study guide. The most important reflection, of course, is the evaluation of the liturgies that congregations are asked to do so that the Standing Liturgical Commission can learn from the experience of the Church. Here the reflection will be done formally, with each person responding to specific questions about experiences of worship with the texts, and then talking together as a congregation to share the reflection experience as a worshiping community.

The Supplemental Liturgical Texts and the whole issue of inclusive language in the Church are controversial. Read the remarks about encouraging dialogue in the first session. Encourage persons to speak out. Acknowledge the controversial nature of the study as you begin the first session so that those who may be upset find recognition for their positions. Emphasize that the Supplemental Liturgical Texts are not a completed package, but are offered to the Church as a way of drawing us into dialogue about the language of our worship. Differing viewpoints are essential. We who are the Church must hear each other — both our ideas and the feelings that lie beneath our ideas. This is one of the concerns that shapes this study guide for the Commentary on Prayer Book Studies 30.

Session One

Purpose of the session: To introduce participants to the concerns that lie behind the Supplemental Liturgical Texts.

Begin the first session by asking persons to join with two other participants and respond to the following questions:

- What is your understanding of "inclusive language," especially as it is applied to the Church today?
- How have you come to that understanding and what are your feelings about inclusive language?
- What do you hope to learn in these sessions?

Allow about ten minutes for this dialogue and then draw people back together. Ask persons to share some of their convictions so that the whole group gets an idea of the concerns and feelings that were raised. List the learning goals on chalk board or newsprint for future reference.

This stage is important. It allows persons to share a part of their story and gives them a sense of being heard and appreciated. We want to begin the study by an experience of hearing each other. We cannot talk about "inclusive language" without being an inclusive caring community. In addition, the questions help to draw participants into the study and to set up a dialogue between what people know and some new thoughts we wish to share.

Each session contains some content material that needs to be shared with participants. The complete text of a brief lecture is included; how the content from the lecture is shared is up to you.

A Suggested Lecture:

The Church's concern for "inclusive language."
Why we have Supplemental Liturgical Texts.

Three concerns lie behind the Supplemental Liturgical Texts:

- The language we use about people
- The role of women in salvation history
- The language we use to name and describe God

1. Language about people

In his introductory article, Dr. Mitchell talks about how language changes over time. For a growing number of persons today, the word "man" or "mankind" no longer includes women. On the whole, this concern was dealt with as the 1979 Book of Common Prayer was developed, though the language of the Rite One texts was not changed because of the concern to keep the texts as close to that of previous Prayer Books as possible.

When the Bible is read in liturgy, there is still a problem, however. Until recently, English translations of the Bible, including the familiar Revised Standard Version, consistently used "man" when the Greek or Hebrew word being translated was inclusive, and means "people." Some recent translations of the Bible, such as the New Jerusalem Bible and the New Revised Standard Version of the Bible (which is to be published in 1990), are careful to render terms that are inclusive in Greek or Hebrew into inclusive terms in the English language. These recent translations do not eliminate all gender-specific masculine language. Where the Greek or Hebrew language is gender specific, the English translation will also be gender specific.

2. The role of women in salvation history

Though women played a crucial role in salvation history, they have tended to become invisible in the memory of the Church. This has happened in no small part because of the way the Lectionary has been formed. For example, in Luke 8:1-3, we learn the names of key women who followed Jesus. "Soon afterward he went on through cities and villages, preaching and bringing the good news of the kingdom of God. And the twelve were with him, and also some women who had been healed of evil spirits and infirmities: Mary, called Magdalene, from whom seven demons had gone out, and Joanna, the wife of Chuza, Herod's steward and Susanna, and many others, who provided for them out of their means." This text is never heard in the Sunday worship of the Church.[**]

Ironically, Matthew 26:6-13 is not included in the Lectionary either, though the closing words of this text make it clear that the evangelist felt the action of the woman was one that must be remembered "wherever the gospel is preached."

> Now when Jesus was at Bethany in the house of Simon the leper, a woman came up to him with an alabaster jar of very expensive ointment, and she poured it on his head, as he sat at table. But when the disciples saw it, they were indignant, saying, "Why this waste? For this ointment might have been sold for a large sum, and given to the poor." But Jesus, aware of this, said to them, "Why do you trouble the woman? For she has done a beautiful thing to me. For you always have the poor with you, but you will not always have me. In pouring this ointment on my body

> she has done it to prepare me for burial. Truly, I say to you, wherever the gospel is preached in the whole world, what she has done will be told in memory of her."

The parallel text in Mark (Mark 14:3-9) is appointed to be read on the Monday of Holy Week, not a time when many of the faithful will be gathered to hear this crucially important text.[***] ("The Feminine as Omitted, Optional, or Alternative Story: A feminist review of the Episcopal Eucharistic Lectionary," an unpublished monograph, Jean Campbell, OSH, 1988).

A new hymn in the 1982 Hymnal proclaims the role of women in salvation history in unmistakable terms.

> The first one ever, oh, ever to know of the birth of Jesus was the Maid Mary, was Mary the Maid of Galilee, and blessed is she, is she who believes . . . The first one ever, oh, ever to know of Messiah, Jesus, when he said, "I am He," was the Samaritan woman who drew from the well . . . The first one ever, oh, ever, to know of the rising of Jesus, his glory to be, were Mary, Joanna, and Magdalene . . . (Hymn 673)

The Supplemental Texts speak to this problem by carefully including women as well as men in the eucharistic prayers. "Through Abraham and Sarah you blessed us with a holy heritage" (First Supplemental Prayer). The Standing Liturgical Commission, working ecumenically, continues to strive for a more inclusive Lectionary, where women's role in salvation history can be affirmed by hearing appropriate texts which, in turn, may influence what we hear in sermon, prayer, and in daily conversation.

3. The language we use to address God and to describe our relationship with God

The "Background" chapter in this Commentary (chapter 1) describes the problem we encounter in this area. A few excerpts follow:

> Whether in prayer or in academic theology, the language in which we speak of God is necessarily metaphorical, or analogical. We cannot use human words to speak of God in the same sense in which we use them to speak of human beings. Even words like "good" and "powerful" mean something different when applied to God. These words are perhaps the best analogies we can find to the divine attributes, but they are not

---

[**] [Editor's Note: With the use of the Revised Common Lectionary, this text is now heard on Proper 6 of Year C.]

[***] [Editor's Note: With the use of the Revised Common Lectionary, this text is now heard on Palm Sunday of Year B.]

exact fits. Any image of God or theological construct we may have is too small, too narrow, and grossly inadequate. Some are more obviously inadequate than others, but when human reason and language have gone as far as they can, there is still further to go and more to comprehend . . .

It is almost impossible for human beings to avoid using anthropomorphic terms in thinking about God, and, even if we are able to avoid such terms in theological discourse, we do not pray to a "prime mover unmoved" or a "first cause uncaused." The more "real" and "personal" our notion of God is, the more anthropomorphic our language is likely to be . . .

The great problem of all the figures, images, and metaphors used in the liturgy is that we begin to forget that they are used analogically, and to think of them as literal descriptions. We think of God as wearing a crown, or carrying a shepherd's crook, or seated on a throne. These mental pictures may be devotionally helpful to us, as long as we remember that they are our images, not pictures of God in the reality and fullness of the divine being. The more apt the metaphor, the more likely we are to forget that it is a metaphor. When Jesus says, "I am the vine," we all recognize that it is a figure of speech, but we are apt to forget that "I and the Father are one" is not a literal description . . .

In fact, many of the images of God used in the liturgy are "masculine," and have been historically conditioned by the patriarchal nature not only of Jewish society, but of much of Christian society. If we believe that this reflects cultural bias, and is not a part of the gospel, then the deliberate introduction of complementary "feminine" images to our worship is desirable.

It is easy to discount the importance of the language we use about God. "What difference does it make?" we may say. "We know that God really isn't an old man in the sky. All this is just a metaphor." But language does shape our understanding both of God and of ourselves in subliminal as well as in conscious ways. The message proclaimed subliminally, over time, is that if God is like a man, then men are more like God than women.

a. Names of God in the Old Testament

God is called by a variety of names in the Old Testament. The primary name is "YHWH," an unpronounceable name based on the words of Moses as he stood before the burning bush.

Then Moses said to God, "If I come to the people of Israel and say to them, 'The God of your fathers has sent me to you,' and they ask me,

'What is his name?' what shall I say to them?" God said to Moses, 'I AM WHO I AM" (Exodus 3:13-14).

"I Am Who I Am" is an etymology for the name that was later adapted into the English language as "Jehovah," or still later, "Yahweh." These names are neither masculine nor feminine, but the title "Adonai" or "Lord" has traditionally been used as a substitute by the Jewish people to avoid speaking the sacred name, Yahweh.

Several other names are given God in the Old Testament. For example, the terms "El" and "Elohim" are both translated as "God" in the English language. "El Shaddai" (God of the mountain) is another name used in some of the sources that fed into the present Old Testament text.

b. Metaphors and Similes

Metaphors for God are abundant in the Old and New Testaments. God is a rock, a shepherd, an eagle, a father. Though masculine similes and metaphors predominate, and are most often heard in the liturgy of the Church, there are feminine similes and metaphors in Scripture, and it is these that the Supplemental Texts have tapped. Here are two examples:

> For a long time I have held my peace, I have kept still and restrained myself; now I will cry out like a woman in travail, I will gasp and pant (Isaiah 42:14).

> As one whom his mother comforts, so will I comfort you; you shall be comforted in Jerusalem (Isaiah 66:13).

The metaphor "Father" is used only a few times in the Old Testament. Jesus' frequent use of the term heightens our awareness of that masculine title. The Lord's Prayer is probably said more times than any other prayer in Christian practice. But Jesus did not limit his terminology to the masculine. "O Jerusalem, Jerusalem, killing the prophets and stoning those who are sent to you! How often would I have gathered your children together as a hen gathers her brood under her wings, and you would not" (Matthew 23:37). In John 3:3-5, Jesus tells Nicodemus that he must be born again. As Nicodemus was born a first time from his mother's womb, so he must be born again in "water and the Spirit." The baptismal font has been characterized as the womb of God. To be baptized is to be born "out of the womb of God."

c. The Holy Spirit

Nancy Hardesty in her book *Inclusive Language in the Church*, writes:

> For those concerned about inclusive language, the Spirit presents several problems — and several solutions. In Hebrew and Aramaic, Jesus' native

tongue, the word for spirit, *ruach*, which also means breath or wind, is feminine in gender. The Greek word, *pneuma*, is neuter. Thus to speak of the Holy Spirit as he is incorrect. We can more accurately speak of the Spirit as she or it (and so pronouns referring to the Spirit should be translated in the Scripture). (*Inclusive Language in the Church*, John Knox Press, 1987, page 53)

d. The Divine Wisdom

The "Background" chapter states: "The figure of Christ as the Divine Wisdom, the Hagia Sophia after whom Constantine named his great church in Constantinople, has a distinguished pedigree, but has not appeared often in liturgical prayer." In late Old Testament writings and in the Apocrypha, God's Wisdom that reaches out with knowledge to inspire the human mind is referred to as a feminine personality. "Wisdom cries aloud in the street; in the markets she raises her voice; on the top of the walls she cries out; at the entrance of the city gates she speaks: 'How long, O simple ones, will you love being simple? How long will scoffers delight in their scoffing and fools hate knowledge?' " (Proverbs 1:20-22). The Canticles added to the Morning Prayer liturgy carry this language further. (Read Canticles 22 and 23, SLT). Reference to the power of God's Wisdom is included in the Second Alternative Eucharistic Prayer: "O God, from before time you made ready the creation. Through your Wisdom, your Spirit moved over the deep and brought to birth the heavens . . ."

There is no question that masculine metaphors vastly outnumber feminine metaphors in the Bible, but this is not hard to understand since the Bible came out of a patriarchal society. Because of the sacred nature of the biblical texts that form our Christian tradition, the Supplemental Liturgical Texts do not eliminate masculine imagery and metaphor, but simply balance them with the feminine metaphors that are a part of our biblical tradition as well.

We are accustomed to thinking of God in the masculine, and yet much of the language in the Book of Common Prayer and Hymnal is neither masculine nor feminine. Many of the Collects address God by describing an attribute of God's character. The language is neutral. On the second Sunday of Advent we hear: "Merciful God, who sent your messengers the prophets to preach repentance and prepare the way for our salvation . ." A Collect heard during the summer begins: "O God, the protector of all who trust in you, without whom nothing is strong, nothing is holy . . ." (BCP, Proper 12, page 231).

The Trinity remains a stumbling block to many. How can we address the Trinitarian understanding of God without using "Father, Son, and Holy Spirit?" Hymn 371, "Thou whose almighty word," is a hymn of praise to the Trinity using "almighty word . . . Thou who didst come to bring on thy redeeming wing . . . Spirit of truth and love" as ways of expressing in song the mystery of the Trinity.

The language of our worship is poetic language; it is language that opens our minds to imagine the unimaginable. God speaks in dreams and visions, but we often respond with a demand for ultimate definitions and answers to our questions of mystery. Jesus answered questions with open-ended stories that often raise more questions. As a biblical people we are to be open to the movement of the Spirit. Our worship needs to reflect both the comfort of God's presence in the world as we know it, and the mystery and awe that comes when we stand with Moses before the burning bush to ask the name of the God who calls us.

Following the talk

Have people return to the same small groups they were a part of at the beginning of the session and ask them to talk together for about twenty minutes. Each group is asked to form:

- two questions
- two concerns
- two new discoveries ("ah-has") heard in the talk

When persons return from the small groups, quickly record on chalkboard or newsprint their questions, concerns and discoveries, then spend the rest of the session sharing them. Persons upset over what has been said in the talk need to be heard and affirmed. Their concerns are important. Whenever viewpoints are shared with feeling, invite persons to tell what led them to their convictions. "What experiences have led you to your present position on this matter?" As stories are told, move beyond conflicting theology to sharing life experiences. It is amazing what happens when people begin to enter into each other's story and to hear themselves share some of the points on their own path to their present positions.

An option: Ask participants to form four groups. Assign each group one of the following biblical texts:

- Canticle 8, BCP page 85 (Exodus 15:1-6, 11-13, 17-18)
- Canticle 22, SLT (Wisdom of Solomon, 10:15-19, 20b-21)
- The Venite, BCP page 82 (Psalm 95:1-7)
- Psalm 46, BCP page 649

Ask each group to focus on these questions:

- How did the psalmist understand God's activity in the world?
- What metaphors, images, and poetic words were used by the psalmist to express this understanding?

- How does the psalmist's experience of God match yours?
- What additional metaphors, images, and words would you add to the psalmist's that reflect your experience?

After thirty minutes, draw participants back together into one large group. Ask each group to share the metaphors and imagery notes from their psalm and additional metaphors and words added from the group discussion. Compare these with those familiar to us from the eucharistic rites and from the talk given as a part of this session.

Session Two

Purpose of the session: To explore the Eucharistic rites in the Book of Common Prayer so that participants can study and experience the Supplemental Liturgical Texts with an understanding of the liturgical tradition out of which they come.

Begin the session with prayer and then invite comments, questions, or concerns that have been raised from the first session.

After the initial discussion, offer a brief lecture based on the following material or from additional sources available to the leader, including sections of this Commentary.

A Suggested Lecture:

A brief course in Prayer Book worship

The Supplemental Liturgical Texts are offered to the Church in this Triennium so that we may evaluate the texts through the experience of worship as well as study. This is an important process, and in order to evaluate the texts well, an appreciation of our liturgical heritage is necessary. Such an appreciation will provide us with an important tool in the evaluation process. With this in mind, the following brief course in Prayer Book worship as it applies to the Holy Eucharist is offered. Much of what is said about eucharistic worship applies as well to the liturgies for Morning and Evening Prayer and the Order of Worship for the Evening.

Louis Weil, Professor of Liturgics at the Church Divinity School of the Pacific, in his book *Gathered to Pray: Understanding Liturgical Prayer*, quotes Justin Martyr, a second century scholar, in the description of an early eucharistic celebration:

> On the day named after the sun, all who live in the city or countryside assemble, and the memoirs of the apostles or the writings of the prophets are read for as long as time allows. When the lector has finished, the president addresses us, admonishing us and exhorting us to imitate the

splendid things we have heard. Then we all stand and pray, and, as we said earlier, when we have finished praying, bread, wine, and water are brought up. The president offers prayers of thanksgiving, according to his ability, and the people give their assent with an "Amen!" Next, the gifts over which the thanksgiving has been spoken are distributed, and each one shares in them, while they are also sent via the deacons to the absent brethren. (Louis Weil, *Gathered to Pray: Understanding Liturgical Prayer*, Cowley Publications, Cambridge, MA, 1986, pages 64-65)

That basic form of the eucharistic liturgy still holds true today. The form is immediately evident as we look at "An Order for Celebrating the Holy Eucharist," BCP pages 400-405. Looking at this Order, we can follow the ancient form of worship and praise as it unfolds.

"The People and Priest Gather in the Lord's Name" and "Proclaim and Respond to the Word of God"

The people gather. The story of God's actions in history and in creation are remembered by the people and interpreted in light of the present moment. The news we hear is good, and we respond to God for the word that shapes our lives as Christians. The response comes in hymns, canticles, and psalms that follow the reading of the texts and that frame our movements from one part of the liturgy to the next.

"The People and Priest Pray for the World and the Church"

Our Episcopal form of worship comes straight out of the Jewish heritage. It was out of this heritage that Jesus spoke and acted. Jews pray out of their story. That is, the story of what God has done in the past leads both to their praise and their prayers.

For example, if I face surgery I will look for a surgeon whose reputation is known. I will hear stories about what that surgeon has done and those stories will lead me to both trust in the surgeon and to ask her to be a part of my healing. When healing comes, I join my voice in praise and another chapter is added to the story. Simply stated, so it is with prayer in the Jewish and Christian tradition. We pray out of the salvation story that is rehearsed each time we gather for Eucharist. We know that we can pray for healing, peace, liberation, and reconciliation because our prayers are informed by stories of healing, peace, liberation, and reconciliation.

"The People and Priest Exchange the Peace"

The prayers lead to the "Exchange of the Peace," an act that recognizes our role as God's people today and an act that confronts us with the words of Jesus that admonish worshipers to come to the altar only when reconciled to one another

(Matthew 5:23-24). If we can't honestly exchange the peace with our neighbor, then we must make peace before we can receive the gift of God's peace.

"The People and Priest Prepare the Table" and "Make Eucharist"

With this action we shift our focus from the Word of God to the Sacrament of the table. The rubrics of the Great Thanksgiving in the Order for Eucharist, Form 2 (BCP pages 404-405), provide us with a detailed outline of the prayer.
(The rubrics of Form 1 are similar, but Form 2 is slightly more flexible.)

(1) "The Celebrant gives thanks to God the Father for his work in creation and his relevation of himself to his people."
(2) "Recalls before God, when appropriate, the particular occasion being celebrated."
(3) "Incorporates or adapts the Proper Preface of the day, if desired."
(4) "If the Sanctus is to be included, it is introduced with these or similar words . . ."
(5) "The Celebrant now praises God for the salvation of the world through Jesus Christ our Lord."
(6) "At the following words concerning the bread, the Celebrant is to hold it, or lay a hand upon it; and at the words concerning the cup, to hold or place a hand upon the cup and any other vessel containing wine to be consecrated." (Here a text is provided to be said by the celebrant. The text includes the institution narrative, a remembrance of Jesus' suffering, death, resurrection, and ascension, a reference to "our sacrifice of praise," and an invocation of the Holy Spirit upon the gifts of bread and wine.)
(7) "The Celebrant then prays that all may receive the benefits of Christ's work, and the renewal of the Holy Spirit."
(8) "The Prayer concludes with these or similar words." (The text of a concluding doxology is provided.)

(It would help to have these eight elements of the eucharistic prayer produced as a handout for participants or written out on chalkboard or newsprint.)
The elements common to all eucharistic prayers do not necessarily fall in the order given here, and in Eucharistic Prayer I, Rite One, there is no thanksgiving expressed for God's work in creation.
The pattern of the first part of the liturgy (the Liturgy of the Word) is repeated in the eucharistic prayer. Our remembrance in the prayer of what God has done through Jesus Christ leads to our thanksgiving and the consecration of our gifts of bread and wine to be the "Sacrament of the Body of Christ and his Blood of the new Covenant" (Eucharistic Prayer B, BCP page 369). The whole prayer is a great act of praise and thanksgiving addressed to God and is spoken "by the Priest in the name of the gathering" (BCP page 401). It is our "sacrifice of praise and thanksgiving" (Eucharistic Prayer A, BCP page 363).

"The People and Priest Share the Gifts of God"

And then "... go forth into the world, rejoicing in the power of the Spirit."

This basic shape of the liturgy lies behind everything we do as we gather to celebrate the Eucharist together. Morning and Evening Prayer are liturgies of praise and prayer that have some of the same elements as the first half of the eucharistic liturgy. In Morning and Evening Prayer, we recall the salvation story. Based on that story we affirm our Baptismal Covenant with God by saying the Apostles' Creed, which leads to our confidence in prayer and our thanksgiving in the joy of God's power in our lives.

Notice that in the early rite of the Church described by Justin Martyr, the "president offers prayers of thanksgiving according to his ability..." There are eight eucharistic prayers in the Book of Common Prayer (counting the two forms outlined in "An Order for Celebrating the Holy Eucharist"), a departure from the practice of authorizing only one eucharistic prayer, as was the custom in earlier Prayer Books. The early Church, however, had as many eucharistic prayers as there were celebrants, though the prayers followed a familiar pattern and were gradually formalized into written texts. Even then, however, there was a rich literature of eucharistic prayers used across the Church.

The language of our worship creates an environment that surrounds us with imagery, poetry, and metaphor, and that shapes our understanding and experience of God. This environment of language exerts a powerful influence on our perception of what it means to be the people of God. We tend to think of environment only in terms of church architecture and the arrangement of the building we worship in. As we study and experience the liturgical rites of the Church, we need to be aware of the environment that is created for us in word and language as well as in architectural style.

Leonel Mitchell states in the "Background" chapter of this Commentary:

> In the 16th century a favorite metaphor for God was King. In 1547, the year of Henry VIII's death, a prayer still in the English Prayer Book addressed God as "high and mighty, King of Kings, Lord of Lords, the only ruler of Princes, who dost from thy throne behold all the dwellers upon earth." In Tudor England this image of God as a monarch on a lofty throne with faithful subjects humbly presenting their petitions and supplications was one which emerged naturally out of that context. It evoked the familiar image of a real royal court. The original metaphor of God as "King of Kings" is biblical, but it is fleshed out with the trappings of Tudor monarchy, and from our perspective it seems to suggest arrogance and unapproachability and thereby distorts the image of God.

The environment of the 16th century liturgy was clearly the royal courtroom. The relationship between God and people was just as clearly that of subjects to their king.

For the remainder of this session, we want to invite you into the environment of the eucharistic prayers and into a closer examination of the ingredients that shape those prayers. This will help to prepare us to experience the Supplemental Texts to be introduced at our next session.

The design of the remainder of the session

Following the talk, ask participants to go into six small groups. Each group is to study one of the eucharistic prayers in the Book of Common Prayer. First, have the group identify the various elements of the prayer using Form 2 in "An Order for Celebrating the Holy Eucharist" as their guide.

Next, have someone read the assigned eucharistic prayer slowly and attentively. Encourage silence at the end of the reading, and then ask persons to respond to the following questions. Have the questions ready on newsprint, chalkboard, or printed on a handout sheet.

- Identify how our relationship with God is expressed through names, images, and metaphors applied to God in this prayer.
- What are we saying about God?
- What are we saying about ourselves?
- What is the "environment" of this prayer?
- How does this prayer relate to your experience of God over the years?
- Identify specific words or phrases in the prayer that lead to your responses.

After about thirty minutes, ask participants to come together in one large group. Record the responses from each of the six groups, asking that they summarize their discussion by reflecting on the environment of the prayer and the major emphasis of the prayer.

Next, briefly outline the tradition that each of the eucharistic prayers represents. The following comments are taken from Leonel Mitchell's *Praying Shapes Believing* (Winston Press, 1985, pages 152-154).

> Eight alternative eucharistic prayers are included in the Book of Common Prayer: two in Rite One, four in Rite Two, and two in An Order for Celebrating the Holy Eucharist . . . Since the prayers are alternatives, they should be examined together. No single prayer can say everything which might be desirable to say in a eucharistic prayer. Each has its own emphases, but collectively the prayers present a balanced picture of eucharistic theology.
>
> Eucharistic Prayers C and D present the most extensive thanksgiving for creation. Eucharistic Prayer I, which has been in the American Prayer Book since 1789, does not mention creation at all, but begins after the

Sanctus by giving thanks for the crucifixion (BCP page 344). This eucharistic prayer's narrowing of focus to the atonement and the consecration of the gifts was typical of the religious climate . . . in the 1549 Prayer Book, on which Eucharistic Prayer I is based. This narrowing must be considered a defect in the prayer, but it can be partially remedied by using the first Preface of the Lord's Day (BCP page 344) whenever possible. Eucharistic Prayer II, a conservative revision of Eucharistic Prayer I by the Standing Liturgical Commission, includes thanksgiving for creation . . . Eucharistic Prayer D, a contemporary ecumenical composition based closely on the 4th century Alexandrian *Anaphora* of St. Basil, gives thanks to God as "fountain of life and source of all goodness."

Eucharistic Prayer C, an original contemporary prayer drafted by Howard E. Galley, includes "galaxies, suns, the planets in their courses, and this fragile earth, our island home" in its catalogue of creation, and gives thanks that God has endowed the human race "with memory, reason, and skill" (BCP page 370). Prayers D and C taken together give substance to the creedal affirmation "We believe in one God, the Father, the Almighty, maker of heaven and earth, and of all that is, seen and unseen" (BCP page 358), and they remind us that creation extends far beyond this planet to "the vast expanse of interstellar space" (BCP page 370). They go on to affirm God's making us "in your own image" and "giving the whole world into our care." They also proclaim creation's revelatory power with the words "your mighty works reveal your wisdom and love" (BCP page 373).

Eucharistic Prayer A "is a modern adaptation of the prayer of previous American Prayer Books and of Prayer I, Rite One . . ." "Eucharistic Prayer B combines the ancient prayer of Hippolytus with a prayer composed for trial use in 1970. The prayer emphasizes God's call, the presence of God's word revealed through the prophets, and the incarnation of the Word in Jesus of Nazareth." (*Commentary on the American Prayer Book*, Marion J. Hatchett, Seabury Press, 1981, pages 374-375)

Invite dialogue with questions:

(1) How does the scholar's explanation match our experience of the prayers?
(2) With which prayer are you most familiar? Why do you think you hear it most frequently?
(3) What prayer or prayers would you like more exposure to?
(4) What have you heard in a new way as we have shared these prayers together?
(5) Time permitting, or as a home assignment, you may want to invite participants to write a eucharistic prayer for your study group based on one of the forms in "An Order for Celebrating the Holy Eucharist." This exercise can be done by individuals or small groups.

Session Three

Purpose of the session: To study the Supplemental Texts and to reflect on the experience in light of our previous study.

In the last session we spoke of the "environment" of the eucharistic prayers in Rite One and Rite Two of the Book of Common Prayer 1979. In this session we will experience the environment of the Supplemental Liturgical Texts through study and worship. (If possible, celebrate the Holy Eucharist using Prayer Book Studies 30. If this is not possible, then read the texts as you would read them in public worship. It is essential that participants experience the texts as prayer rather than only study them as documents.)

As an option, begin the celebration or session with the singing of Hymn 371, "Thou, whose almighty word." This hymn of praise uses a variety of images to describe the Trinity, rather than the familiar "Father, Son, and Holy Spirit," as a reminder that we are more accustomed than we might realize to using "inclusive" terminology to describe our understanding of God.

At the conclusion of the celebration or reading, encourage a time of silent reflection. Then ask for immediate responses from participants and record them. Try to avoid conversation, questions, or challenges to what is said. Rather; simply let people speak. Hear what is said and record it so that participants have a sense for the whole experience as it has been described by a variety of people.

Next, ask each participant to respond to the following questions in silence. (These questions need to be prepared as a handout sheet for each person, though in smaller settings the questions could simply be posted on newsprint or chalkboard.)

- What feelings did the experience of the Supplemental Texts raise in you?
- Please try to identify specific things in the service that caused these feelings (i.e. words, phrases, images).
- What thoughts did the use of the Supplemental Liturgical Texts raise in you?
- Please try to identify specific things in the text that stimulated these thoughts.
- What was the "environment" of the eucharistic prayer for you?

After about fifteen minutes, ask participants to form groups of no more than four persons. Each participant is to share his or her responses to the questions, and each group is to prepare a succinct statement that captures some of the concerns and feelings raised. An option would be to ask the groups to first identify the common elements of each eucharistic prayer based on the discussion during the last session.

In the total group hear the reports from the small groups. Reports need to be limited to one or two comments under each of the categories on the evaluation sheet. If comments have already been made in a previous group, simply affirm that fact.

Finally, compare words, phrases, and metaphors from the Supplemental Liturgical Texts with those found in the six eucharistic prayers of the BCP.

Next, lead participants through the Daily Office section of Prayer Book Studies 30. By highlighting the following portions of the texts, participants will have a feeling for the approach taken in the Daily Office, Rite Two, Adapted.

In Morning Prayer: Rite Two Adapted:

(1) The alternative to the opening versicle, page 9-10.
(2) The alternative to the Gloria Patri, page 10.
(3) Compare the alternative to the Invitatory Psalms, Psalm 63, SLT page 12-13, with the Invitatory Psalms, BCP pages 82-83.
(4) Read Canticle 8, The Song of Moses, BCP page 85, and compare it with Canticle 22, SLT page 20.
(5) The alternative to the salutation ("Hear our cry, O God . . .") SLT page 21.
(6) Suffrages B, SLT page 22. (Suffrages are prayer petitions using versicles said by the leader with responses said by the congregation. The Suffrages of Morning Prayer are composed of verses from the Psalter.)
(7) Compare the Collect for the Renewal of Life, BCP page 99, with the same prayer, SLT page 23-24.

In An Order of Worship for the Evening Adapted:

(1) The alternative blessing, SLT page 30.

In Evening Prayer: Rite Two Adapted:

(1) Compare the alternative versicle ("O God, be not far from us. Come quickly to help us, O God.") with the versicle from the Book of Common Prayer. See SLT page 30 and BCP page 117.
(2) Compare the first prayer for mission, SLT page 38, with the same prayer, BCP page 124.
(3) Compare the Prayer of St. Chrysostom, SLT page 39, with the same prayer, BCP page 126. Note the comment in Chapter Two of this Commentary: "A new rendering of the Greek text. English versions of this prayer have always been problematical, and it is suspected by some scholars that Archbishop Cranmer may have had a defective text before him. The Greek is based on Matthew 18:19, which specifically speaks of *agreeing*, and not just *gathering*, as the basis for our requests being answered. The Greek, moreover, is addressed to Christ, as is Cranmer's translation." Here we see an example of the concern expressed throughout the Supplemental Texts to honor the tradition from which our prayers come. In some cases, the Supplemental Liturgical Texts

return to an earlier tradition of the Church's prayer than has been expressed in the current and previous editions of the Book of Common Prayer.

As each portion of the adapted Daily Office is studied, use the following procedure to examine the texts:

(1) Read the text prayerfully as if you are reading it in public worship.
(2) Read the comparative text from the Book of Common Prayer in the same way.
(3) Ask participants to point out the differences. Ask:
- Why do you think the changes were made?
- How do the new texts sound to you?
- How do you feel about them?
- What questions are raised for you?

Encourage discussion.

Conclude this study series by briefly discussing the principles that lie behind the work of the Committee on Supplemental Liturgical Texts of the Standing Liturgical Commission.

Principles that Guide the Work of the Committee on Supplemental Liturgical Texts

Four principles lie behind the work of the Committee on Supplemental Liturgical Texts. First, the Supplemental Eucharistic Prayers continue the principle begun in the development of the present Book of Common Prayer. To quote from Dr. Mitchell's *Praying Shapes Believing*, "No single prayer can say everything which might be desirable to say in a eucharistic prayer. Each has its own emphases, but collectively the prayers present a balanced picture of eucharistic theology." In other words, no one prayer can capture the fullness of our rich liturgical heritage. The second principle follows from this statement. The two eucharistic prayers, along with the Liturgy of the Word, that are offered in Prayer Book Studies 30, placed alongside the eucharistic prayers of the Book of Common Prayer, offer an "inclusive" experience of worship in which feminine as well as masculine imagery for God is expressed in the worship of the Church. The fullness of our biblical and liturgical tradition is expressed as the congregation experiences the variety of prayers over time. It is the balance of the prayers that provides the fullness of imagery that we seek rather than an attempt to neutralize the language we use about God. This concept has been referred to as "complementarity." (Robert L. Hurd, "Complementarity: A Proposal for Liturgical Language," *Worship*, Volume 61, Number 5, September 1987, pages 386-405).

The third principle has already been inferred. The imagery and metaphors that we use to describe our relationship with God must come from the tradition;

it is the Bible and the liturgical heritage of the Church that shapes our present language of prayer.

A final principle is that language about people will always be inclusive. Additionally, the Commission and Committee committed themselves to the long-term task of allowing supplemental prayers to reflect the varieties of human cultures and communities whose voices are increasingly contributing to the life of the Episcopal Church.

Conclude the session by offering the blessing from An Order of Worship for the Evening: "May the blessing of the God of Abraham and Sarah, and of Jesus Christ born of our sister Mary, and of the Holy Spirit, who broods over the world as a mother over her children, be upon you and remain with you always."

Evaluation of the Course

Allow time at the last session for evaluation. The evaluation helps your diocesan and congregational team know what kind of support is needed during the time the Supplemental Texts are being used. Comments forwarded to your diocesan office will help improve the education programs in the future.

(1) How have these sessions fulfilled or not fulfilled your hopes expressed at the beginning of the first session?

(2) What was most/least helpful to you?

(3) What do you need now to more fully understand the Supplemental Liturgical Texts?

(4) How have your feelings and understandings of the Supplemental Liturgical Texts changed (or not changed) as a result of your participation in these sessions?

(5) What are some discoveries about the worship practices of the Episcopal Church for you?

Important Note

The Supplemental Texts are in the process of on-going revision.

Your parish and diocese are also asked to participate in the evaluation of the Texts being conducted by the Liturgical Commission. Inquiries about the process should be directed to the Bishop's office of your Diocese.

Preparing Children for Praying with the Supplemental Liturgical Texts

From time to time, children need to explore the language and power of the liturgical tradition of which they are a part. The Supplemental Liturgical Texts provide a vehicle for that study. The following study guide follows the same three-session pattern as the adult program and is designed for children from about the third grade through the eighth grade. Help younger children to feel at home with the Book of Common Prayer by guiding them through the actions of the liturgy (praise, hearing the story, prayer, etc.) and by rehearsing the liturgical responses with them. If your congregation is going to use the Supplemental Liturgical Texts, introduce them and rehearse those parts of the texts that the children will be saying together in worship.

Each session is divided into four parts. (1) *Beginning the session* offers a way to catch the attention of the children. (2) *Telling the story* is a brief talk that offers content that is important to share with children. (3) *Exploring the story* provides an opportunity for the children to interact with the content through discussion, study, and an activity. (4) *Concluding the session* gives a brief way to summarize and conclude the class time.

The designs are based on about a fifty-minute class time. We realize that this may not be a realistic expectation for many congregations with sporadic church school attendance and thirty to forty minute class times. Consider the following:

- Promote the program by pointing out the importance of preparation for both children and adults.
- Hold the adult's and children's sessions during the same three weeks so that parents make a commitment to participate along with their children.
- Extend the church school class sessions temporarily. Offer a continental breakfast for adults and children as a way of encouraging participation.
- Offer the study on three succeeding weeknights with adult sessions held concurrently.
- Include parents and children together in an intergenerational study.

If the study time comes before the Sunday or a weeknight liturgy, participants will have the opportunity to prepare for the worship experience through their participation in the study sessions.

Session One:
The language of our worship

Purpose of the session:
To explore the language we use to describe our relationship with God so that children can be more aware of the metaphors they hear in the Bible, the Book of Common Prayer, and in the Supplemental Liturgical Texts.

Beginning the session:
Before the children arrive, make a display of pictures illustrating some of the following metaphors for God found in the Psalter. God as

- righteous judge — Psalm 7:12
- governor — Psalm 8:1
- shepherd — Psalm 23:1
- a friend — Psalm 25:13
- light — Psalm 27:1
- a shield — Psalm 28:8
- a safe refuge — Psalm 28:10
- a castle — Psalm 31:3
- a king — Psalm 47:7
- a helper — Psalm 54:4
- a great bird — Psalm 57:1, Psalm 61:4
- a stronghold — Psalm 59:19
- a strong tower against an enemy — Psalm 61:3
- a crag — Psalm 71:3
- the sun — Psalm 84:10
- a shield — Psalm 84:10
- a father — Psalm 89:26
- a protecting bird — Psalm 91:4
- a rock — Psalm 95:1
- a song — Psalm 118:14
- a lantern — Psalm 119:105 (God's word)

As a group, talk about these metaphors. What do they tell us about how our biblical ancestors felt about God?

Telling the story: (Brief talk)
Read over the talk included in the first adult session and Dr. Mitchell's introductory article. Prepare your own brief talk for the children. Most of the images we apply to God are masculine, but some of those from the Psalms could be either masculine or feminine. In addition, there is language for God in the Bible that is distinctly feminine. The Supplemental Liturgical Texts emphasize that feminine biblical imagery — thus providing a more balanced way of expressing our relationship with God. Some of these are:

> *Proverbs 3:13-20 and 8:1-5* (God's wisdom is spoken of as a woman offering the great gift of knowledge).
> *Isaiah 66:13* "As one whom his mother comforts, so I will comfort you; you shall be comforted in Jerusalem."
> *Isaiah 42:14* "For a long time I have held my peace, I have kept still and restrained myself; now I will cry out like a woman in travail, I will gasp and pant."

Isaiah 49:15 "Can a woman forget her sucking child, that she should have no compassion on the son of her womb? Even these may forget, yet I will not forget you."

Matthew 23:37 "O Jerusalem, Jerusalem, killing the prophets and stoning those who are sent to you! How often would I have gathered your children together as a hen gathers her brood under her wings, but you would not!"

Luke 15:8-10 "What woman, having ten silver coins, if she loses one coin, does not light a lamp and sweep the house and seek diligently until she finds it? And when she has found it, she calls together her friends and neighbors, saying, 'Rejoice with me, for I have found the coin which I had lost.' Just so, I tell you, there is joy before the angels of God over one sinner who repents."

What do these passages add to our picture of God's love for us and our need to respond to God? Emphasize with the children that metaphors and poetic images are ways that we describe the relationship we feel with God. God cannot possibly be defined in human or literal terms and our metaphorical language changes over time as our relationship with God deepens. The wide range of imagery found in the Psalms helps us appreciate the depth and range of the relationship these poets felt with God. The same depth of experience and expression is part of the Church today.

Exploring the story:
Go back to the metaphors discussed at the beginning of the session. Point to several of them and ask what each one says about God in specific terms. Example: a rock denotes stability and trust. How would the children use that word to describe people they know? Use each one in a sentence. "Sally is like a rock. When you need a friend whom you can count on, you can count on her."

Can the children think of any new metaphors that help them describe how they feel about God? Encourage them to come up with their own list of metaphors and images that would not have been known in biblical times.

If your church building has stained glass windows and other works of art, take the children on a tour of the church, or show children pictures from a well illustrated book of Christian art. How does the art we see in a church building or book express our relationship with God? What metaphors do we see depicted? (Example: Jesus as the good shepherd)

If time permits, have children create a mural depicting images of God using a large sheet of butcher paper and magic markers or paints.

Concluding the session:
Close the session by encouraging children to listen for language in the worship service that describes our relationship with God. Point out a few examples of what they will hear at the Eucharist. Example: What metaphors do we hear in

the "Glory to God in the highest"? Or the "Song to the Lamb"? (used in place of the Gloria in PBS 30).

Session Two

Purpose of the session:
To explore the eucharistic rites in the Book of Common Prayer so that children will have a deeper appreciation for the liturgy of the Church.

Beginning the session:
Decorate the classroom as if you were having a formal dinner. Put a tablecloth on the table with candles. As children gather, talk about what we do when we share a dinner together such as on Thanksgiving Day. List the activities the children name.

- Option: Use a party setting and talk about what happens when people get together to celebrate a special occasion.

Telling the story:
Adapt the lecture material provided for the adults in the second session so that children can have their own tour through the eucharistic rites of the Book of Common Prayer. Where applicable, refer to activities we do in the Eucharist with what families and friends do when they gather for a meal. (Bring gifts, tell stories. . .) Use "An Order for Celebrating the Holy Eucharist" as the vehicle for studying the other eucharistic texts. Quote the description of an early eucharist by Justin Martyr found at the start of Session 2 in the Study Guide and talk about the structure of the eucharistic rite that is still followed by the Church to this day. The early Church had as many eucharistic prayers as there were celebrants, but today we have eight prayers in the Book of Common Prayer (two in Rite One, four in Rite Two and two in "An Order for Celebrating the Holy Eucharist"). Each prayer expresses our thanksgiving to God in a different way.

Responding to the story:
Have the children count off from one to six as a way of forming six different groups. Using Handout #1 printed at the end of this session, have each group look at the paragraph from one of the eucharistic prayers. Each group will need the leadership of a youth or an adult.

- The leader shows the children the content of each segment of the prayer as it is printed in the Book of Common Prayer. "This is the opening paragraph of the eucharistic prayer. It gives thanks for God's power revealed in creation, in history, and most especially in Jesus."
- The leader asks the children: "What is the main idea expressed in the opening paragraph of this prayer? What does it emphasize about God's action in history and creation?"

- How do you know that what you have said is the main idea expressed in this paragraph? What are the "clincher" sentences or words?
- What words do you need help with?

After fifteen minutes, ask the children to come back together as a total group again.

Ask each group to

- Share words they need help with. Leaders will need to prepare definitions ahead of time. Two helpful resources are *Words of Our Worship* and *A New Dictionary for Episcopalians*. (See bibliography)
- Record on newsprint or chalkboard responses from each group.
- The main idea in Eucharistic Prayer I, Rite One is:
- Words that stood out for us are:
- Quickly go through the other five prayers asking each group to respond to the same questions.
- When all six groups have reported, point out the different emphases in the six prayers. Talk about the differences in each prayer. Explain that at the next session the children will hear two new prayers that they can compare with the prayers they have already studied. (Be sure to save the responses from this session for use at the next session.)

Look at the bulletin for the liturgy this Sunday. What eucharistic prayer will we be using today? Is it the one with which we are most familiar? What is our psalm today and what form of the Prayers of the People will we be using?

If there is time, have children make bookmarks with the titles, *The Psalm, Prayers of the People, Eucharistic Prayer*, printed on them. Referring to the bulletin, have children place the markers in the appropriate place in their Prayer Books as an additional way of preparing for worship.

- Question: What will children tell their parents about the Book of Common Prayer as they go home today?

Session Three

Purpose:
To introduce participants to the Supplemental Liturgical Texts.

Beginning the session:
Post the newsprint sheets with the prayer comparisons from the last session. Begin the session by reading each of the portions of the eucharistic prayers shared last week from the handout. Then read the same portions of the First and Second Supplemental Prayers from the Supplemental Liturgical Texts, giving each child

a copy of Handout #2. What is the main idea in each of these paragraphs taken from these two prayers? What does each prayer emphasize about God's action in history and in creation? What words stand out for the children as they hear the new texts? Record their responses and compare them with what was said about the six eucharistic prayers from the Book of Common Prayer.

Telling the Church's story:
Lead the children through the whole eucharistic rite from the opening acclamation at the beginning of the liturgy through the dismissal, using one of the Supplemental Eucharistic Prayers for your study. Have them repeat the congregational responses several times so that they grow accustomed to them. Compare the eucharistic prayers from the Supplemental Liturgical Texts with one of the eucharistic prayers from the Book of Common Prayer. Point out similarities and differences. Encourage the children to ask questions including the meaning of words and terms. Use the "Introduction to the Supplemental Texts" (Chapter 2) as the basis for your remarks to the children, picking five or six highlights that you feel may be significant.

Exploring the story:
Have the children write parts of a eucharistic prayer following the rubrics on page 404-405, Form 2, "An Order for Celebrating the Holy Eucharist." Write the rubrics and questions on newsprint or prepare them as a handout for each child. Use the rubrics and the questions that go with them as a basis for discussion. Take note of what is shared.

- *The Celebrant gives thanks to God the Father for his work in creation and his revelation of himself to his people.*

    Ask: What are we excited about as we think about the wonderful world and our lives that God has given us?

- *Recalls before God, when appropriate, the particular occasion being celebrated.*

    Ask: What do we want to celebrate as we think about the things we have shared together as a class or as a member of our Church this year?

    The Celebrant now praises God for the salvation of the world through Jesus Christ our Lord.

    Ask: What have we seen happening in our lives that reminds us of events that happened in Jesus' time? (healing, love shared, stories told, people's lives changed, etc.)

- (At the end of the prayer) *The Celebrant then prays that all may receive the benefits of Christ's work, and the renewal of the Holy Spirit.*

    Ask: What do we want to pray will happen for God's world, for the Church, for ourselves as a result of the power of God's love made known to us as we celebrate the Holy Eucharist together?

Use the ideas generated by the children's discussion to write a simple prayer that follows the outline of the rubrics. Explain to the children that if you added the words found in Form or Form 2 in "An Order for Celebrating the Holy Eucharist" (pages 403 and 405) you would have your own eucharistic prayer that you could use as a class in celebrating the eucharist together.

Concluding the session:
Read the prayer the children have participated in writing as a closing prayer of thanksgiving.

Handout #1

Selected Portions Six Eucharistic Prayers Book of Common Prayer

Eucharistic Prayer 1, Rite One, page 334, Group One

All glory be to thee, Almighty God, our heavenly Father, for that thou, of thy tender mercy, didst give thine only Son Jesus Christ to suffer death upon the cross for our redemption; who made there, by his one oblation of himself once offered, a full, perfect, and sufficient sacrifice, oblation, and satisfaction, for the sins of the whole world; and did institute, and in his holy Gospel command us to continue, a perpetual memory of that his precious death and sacrifice, until his coming again.

Eucharistic Prayer II, Rite One, page 341

All glory be to thee, O Lord our God, for that thou didst create heaven and earth, and didst make us in thine own image; and, of thy tender mercy, didst give thine only Son Jesus Christ to take our nature upon him, and to suffer death upon the cross for our redemption. He made there a full and perfect sacrifice for the whole world; and did institute, and in his holy Gospel command us to continue, a perpetual memory of that his precious death and sacrifice, until his coming again.

Eucharistic Prayer A, Rite Two, page 362

Holy and gracious Father: In your infinite love you made us for yourself; and, when we had fallen into sin and become subject to evil and death, you, in your mercy, sent Jesus Christ, your only and eternal Son, to share our human nature, to live and die as one of us, to reconcile us to you, the God and Father of all.

    He stretched out his arms upon the cross, and offered himself, in obedience to your will, a perfect sacrifice for the whole world.

Eucharistic Prayer B, Rite Two, page 368

We give thanks to you, O God, for the goodness and love which you have made known to us in creation; in the calling of Israel to be your people; in your Word spoken through the prophets; and above all in the Word made flesh, Jesus, your Son. For in these last days you sent him to be incarnate from the Virgin Mary, to be the Savior and Redeemer of the world. In him, you have delivered us from evil, and made us worthy to stand before you. In him, you have brought us out of error into truth, out of sin into righteousness, out of death into life.

Eucharistic Prayer C, Rite Two, page 370

God of all power, Ruler of the Universe, you are worthy of glory and praise.
Glory to you for ever and ever.

At your command all things came to be: the vast expanse of interstellar space, galaxies, suns, the planets in their courses, and this fragile earth, our island home.
By your will they were created and have their being.

From the primal elements you brought forth the human race, and blessed us with memory, reason, and skill. You made us the rulers of creation. But we turned against you, and betrayed your trust; and we turned against one another.
Have mercy, Lord, for we are sinners in your sight.

Again and again, you called us to return. Through prophets and sages you revealed your righteous Law. And in the fullness of time you sent your only Son, born of a woman, to fulfill your Law, to open for us the way of freedom and peace.
By his blood, he reconciled us.
By his wounds, we are healed.

And therefore we praise you, joining with the heavenly chorus, with prophets, apostles, and martyrs, and with all those in every generation who have looked to you in hope, to proclaim with them your glory, in their unending hymn.

Eucharistic Prayer D, Rite Two, page 373-374

We acclaim you, holy Lord, glorious in power. Your mighty works reveal your wisdom and love. You formed us in your own image, giving the whole world into our care, so that, in obedience to you, our Creator, we might rule and serve all your creatures. When our disobedience took us far from you, you did not abandon us to the power of death. In your mercy you came to our help, so that in seeking you we might find you. Again and again you called us into covenant with you, and through the prophets you taught us to hope for salvation.

Father, you loved the world so much that in the fullness of time you sent your only Son to be our Savior. Incarnate by the Holy Spirit, born of the Virgin Mary, he lived as one of us, yet without sin. To the poor he proclaimed the good news of salvation; to prisoners, freedom; to the sorrowful, joy. To fulfill your purpose he gave himself up to death; and, rising from the grave, destroyed death, and made the whole creation new.

And, that we might live no longer for ourselves, but for him who died and rose for us, he sent the Holy Spirit, his own first gift for those who believe, to complete his work in the world, and to bring to fulfillment the sanctification of all.

Handout #2

Selected Portions Eucharistic Prayers Supplemental Liturgical Texts

First Supplemental Eucharistic Prayer, page 46-47

It is good and joyful that in your presence we give you thanks, Holy God, for you have included us in creation and made us in your glorious image. You have remembered us from our beginning and fed us with your constant love; you have redeemed us in Jesus Christ and knit us into one body. Through your Spirit you replenish us, and call us to fullness of life. Therefore, joining with angels and archangels and with all the faithful in every generation, we give voice to all creation as we sing (say): Holy, holy . . .

Most generous, self-giving God,
we celebrate your gift of creation.
We rejoice that you have formed us in your image
and called us to dwell in your infinite love.

You gave the world into our care
that we might be your faithful stewards
and reflect your bountiful grace.
Through Abraham and Sarah
you blessed us with a holy heritage.
You delivered us from slavery,
sustained us in the wilderness,
and raised up prophets
that we might realize the fullness of your promise.

But we failed to honor your image
in one another and in ourselves;
we failed to see your goodness in the world around us;
and so we violated your creation,
abused one another,
and rejected your love.

Yet you did not abandon us to sin and death,
but sent Jesus Christ to be our Savior.

United with us by incarnation
through Mary and the Holy Spirit,
and born into the human family,
he showed us the way of freedom and life.
Walking among us,
he touched us with healing and transforming power,
and showed us your glory
Giving himself freely to death on the cross,
he triumphed over evil and became our salvation.

Second Supplemental Eucharistic Prayer, page 50

O God, from before time you made ready the creation. Through your Wisdom, your Spirit moved over the deep and brought to birth the heavens: sun, moon, and stars; earth, winds, and waters; growing things, both plants and animals; and finally humankind. You made us in your image, male and female, to love and care for the earth and its creatures as you love and care for us, your children.

You graced us with freedom of heart and mind, but we were heedless and willful. You took us by the hand, and taught us to walk in your ways. And though you led us with cords of compassion and bands of love, we wandered far away. Yet as a mother cares for her children, you would not forget us. Time and again you called us to live in the fullness of your love.

Then you acted anew in Creation. In order that we might see and know the riches of your grace, your Spirit entered into Mary, the maiden of Nazareth, that she might conceive and bear a Son, the holy child of God.

Bibliography

Books

Guilbert, Charles Mortimer, *Words of Our Worship: A Practical Liturgical Dictionary*; The Church Hymnal Corporation, 1988

Hardesty, Nancy, A., *Inclusive Language in the Church*; John Knox Press, 1987

Hatchett, Marion J., *Commentary on the American Prayer Book*; The Seabury Press, 1980

Jasper, R.C. David & G.J. Cuming, *Prayers and the Eucharist: Early and Reformed*; Pueblo Publishing Co., 3rd revised edition, 1987

Mitchell, Leonel L., *The Meaning of Ritual*; Morehouse Barlow, 1977

Mitchell, Leonel L., *Praying Shapes Believing: A Theological Commentary on the Book of Common Prayer*; Winston Press, 1985

Ramshaw, Gail, *Christ in Sacred Speech: The Meaning of Liturgical Language*; Fortress Press, 1986

Russell, Letty M., *The Liberating Word: A Guide to Nonsexist Interpretation of the Bible*; The Westminster Press, 1976

Schneiders, Sandra M., *Women and the Word*; Paulist Press, 1986

Senn, Frank C., ed., *New Eucharistic Prayers: An Ecumenical Study of Their Development and Structure*; Paulist Press, 1987

Standing Liturgical Commission, *The Occasional Papers of the Standing Liturgical Commission: Collection Number One*; The Church Hymnal Corporation

Stevick, Daniel B., *Baptismal Moments; Baptismal Meanings*; The Church Hymnal Corporation, 1987

Stuhlman, Byron D., *Prayer Book Rubrics Expanded*; The Church Hymnal Corporation, 1987

Trible, Phyllis, *God and the Rhetoric of Sexuality*; Fortress Press, 1978

Wall, John N., Jr., *A New Dictionary for Episcopalians*; Winston Press, 1985

Weil, Louis, *Gathered to Pray: Understanding Liturgical Prayer: A Parish Life Sourcebook*; Cowley Publications & Forward Movement Publications, 1986

Weil, Louis, *Sacraments and Liturgy: The Outward Signs*; Basil Blackwell, Inc., 1983

Periodicals:

Procter-Smith, Marjorie, "Liturgical Anamnesis and Women's Memory: Something Missing," pp. 405-414, *Worship*, Vol. 61, Number 5, September, 1987

Hurd, Robert L., "Complementarity: A Proposal for Liturgical Language," pp. 386-405, *Worship*, Vol. 61, Number 5, September, 1987

Westerhoff, John H. III, ed., *Religious Education*, Vol. 80, Number 4, Fall, 1985 (Issue on Inclusive Language)

Study Guide:

Geitz, Elizabeth, and Prescott, Margaret, "Recovering Lost Tradition: Exploring the Supplemental Liturgical Texts with a Pastoral and Historical Approach," Trinity Church, Princeton, Diocese of New Jersey, 1989.

www.ingramcontent.com/pod-product-compliance
Lightning Source LLC
Chambersburg PA
CBHW061350300426
44116CB00011B/2066